AIR POLLUTION IN IRELAND
DUBLIN
A CASE STUDY

A publication derived from the Royal Dublin Society Seminar held on
November 30, 1985

Edited by

CHARLES MOLLAN & JAMES WALSH

ROYAL DUBLIN SOCIETY
1988

THE ROYAL DUBLIN SOCIETY
acknowledges the generous financial assistance of

ALLIED IRISH BANKS plc
BORD GAIS EIREANN
COAL ADVISORY BOARD
ELECTRICITY SUPPLY BOARD
ESSO IRELAND LIMITED
HIBERNIAN INSURANCE plc
IRISH LIFE ASSURANCE plc
IRISH NATIONAL INSURANCE COMPANY plc
NEW DUBLIN GAS
ULSTER BANK LIMITED

towards the costs of the Seminar and
the publication of this volume

Cover design by Alan Corsini

Typeset and printed in the Republic of Ireland by
Mount Salus Press Limited, Dublin

CONTENTS

INTRODUCTION

The Seminar, "Air Pollution in Ireland — Dublin — A Case Study", organised by the Science Committee of the Royal Dublin Society, was designed to review Dublin air quality, as well as effects of pollutants on both materials and human health. It was strategically timed, so that the conclusions could be taken into account by those shaping our first comprehensive piece of air quality management legislation — the Air Pollution Bill 1986 — on its passage through Senate and Dail. The Proceedings of this Seminar, however, are now published after the Bill has passed into law. Thus you, the reader, can get a picture of where environmental quality control has gone wrong in the past; but, more important, you can be pointed to a new way which could be paved by the Air Pollution Act if it is properly implemented. Personally, I believe that such implementation depends largely on public participation in environmental management. A short resumé of the backdrop to Dublin's air quality today should highlight the basis for this opinion.

Since 1973, we have had a Dublin Corporation monitoring network with the data gathered reflecting a steadily improving and, by international standards, rather good urban air quality. Even so, John O'Leary, Minister of State at the Department of the Environment, at his opening address to the last major Air Pollution Seminar in 1978, indicated that we could not afford to be complacent. He also mentioned the preparation of a National Environment Policy as one of the most important functions of the Minister, and finally noted: "there should be well-informed public opinion on the whole question of air pollution". Ireland seemed set on the right road.

But then the 1979 oil crises triggered government incentives towards coal. Increased coal sales were paralleled by increased smoke emissions. The January 1982 smog episode doubled mortality rates at St James's Hospital, and we can assume, from the study carried out for this Hospital, that other hospitals had corresponding experiences. Medical warnings of bronchitis and chest ailments began a questioning of a fuel policy which favoured coal. By the end of 1982, the gas pipeline to Dublin was completed, but coal sales continued to rise.

On April 1, 1983, the Council of the European Communities smoke and SO_2 Directive came into force. However, as Ireland asked for (and was granted) a 10 year derogation for Dublin, this piece of legislation appeared to have no impact on government grants for chimneys, or on the backboiler and open fire place policy in local authority housing. In the same year Warren Spring Laboratories undertook a consultancy study for Dublin Corporation which included air pollution modelling. The results were clear: based on our fuel mix policy, the consultants predicted that more than half of the monitoring sites in the city would break the EEC Directive smoke limit values by 1990/91. The report again stated that smokey fuel in domestic fires was the main source of air pollution. Yet, in the first annual report to the EEC, published in 1985, the Irish Government contribution on counter measures to Dublin smoke pollution read: "investigations into the reasons are underway, including the application of mathematical models".

In the United Kingdom, it was shown that there was a strong correlation between increase in smoke control and decrease in domestic coal consumption — as Williams has pointed out in his paper (p 51). So, in Ireland, the coal industry launched an effective sales campaign equating home with a warm coal fire. An information booklet was also published indicating, among other things, that, although coal sales increased in the winter of 1985/6, there was a 15% fall in winter median city smoke levels. This, it was argued, showed that the main cause for smoke pollution must not be coal.

However, wind speed analyses show that 1985/86 was abnormally windy, with only eleven hours of calm recorded in the five month period November to March. I suggest that it was this factor which reduced the air pollution due to domestic coal fires.

An article in *The Irish Times,* published just before the RDS Seminar, identified areas which suffered effects of poverty and deprivation in Dublin "the divided city". If you turn to Bailey's map of smoke emission zones in this book (p 25), you can largely replace his high pollutant emission zones by those identified in the article as underprivileged. Inadequate dispersion of smoke from low domestic chimneys ensures that such areas are particularly subject to their own pollution. So why do the people who suffer most not change to clean gas? Do they believe coal is cheaper? Or are they attracted to the magic of a real coal fire? One may argue that those on coal vouchers cannot afford to install gas heating, but why are there no protest marches in areas of high pollution demanding help, and why was there almost nobody at the RDS Seminar from high pollution areas?

The reason, I believe, is that we have collectively failed:
—as scientists to demand and give sufficient information;
—as educators to highlight such environmental, health, and consumer issues;
—as coal industry to promote smokeless fuel;
—as elected representatives to do all that is in our power to protect, inform, and assist those least able to change things for themselves;
—as individuals to take more interest, feel more responsible for our own and our elected representatives' actions.

Fuel Substitution

At the Seminar, it was emphasised that action on fuel substitution was most urgent. Methods suggested ranged from total prohibition of smokey coal, peat, and wood in all urban households, to provision of smokeless zones in the City, to positive incentives such as grants for clean fuel and appliances. In principle, any of those methods of fuel substitution put forward could be applied under the Air Pollution Act. Article 23 enables the Minister for the Environment to prohibit specified emissions, with Article 25 focussing on smoke emission control from any premises. However, this may be difficult to enforce if it is not combined with financial backing as, in any prosecution, it shall be good defence to demonstrate that the "best practicable means" had been used to limit smoke emissions — and this includes cost considerations of renovating the facilities to reduce smoke. Article 53 looks potentially far more effective in achieving quick fuel substitution, as it gives the Minister power to regulate import markets and even use of potentially polluting fuels.

Local authorities broadly have the same power to prohibit emissions from premises, as has the Minister (Article 26) — though there is more detail on the mechanisms of directing an occupier of a premises to undertake required action in a given time.

Special Control Areas (SCAs), asked for by so many RDS Seminar speakers, are also provided for. An SCA order may be drawn up by a local authority for a specified area with air quality problems. Under the order, a range of options to limit air pollution is listed, including the prohibition of certain fireplaces.

There are, however, rights of objection which, if used, demand an oral hearing. This in turn demands a report with recommendations to be taken into account by the Minister before he gives his final approval for an SCA order. Once that is achieved, there is a minimum wait of six months before the order can come into operation (Article 41).

Thus an SCA hinges on three points:
1. What air quality levels are aimed for?
2. What are the emission control options?
3. What costs are involved and for whom?

A very soft SCA order favouring the installation of smoke reducing appliances (by giving a grant just high enough for the new coal heaters but not sufficient for gas installation) should be acceptable to the coal industry and suit our own peat briquette sales. An order aiming for the higher standards obtained by a greater conversion to gas would meet with strong coal industry objections. Such objections should not be under-estimated, bearing in mind some of the amendments pushed through in the course of the Air Pollution Bill debate (eg, occupiers of private dwellings now need 24 hours written notice before an authorised person can enter the premises to check fuel used).

In my opinion, it is unlikely that a **strong** SCA order would be in force before 1990 in even the most smog prone areas of Dublin, and hence it is well to base calls for action on Article 27, which allows local authorities to take urgent measures to prevent air pollution without notices, orders, or other time-consuming obstacles.

Public Information

Stressing, as I do, the importance of public participation in environmental management, it is clear that we need ready access to raw data such as gathered by the Dublin Corporation Air Pollution Monitoring Unit. We need immediate access to surveys, models or reports made for local authorities or state bodies. We need to know the terms of licenses as well as tender details for industrial plant. Much of this we could be legally entitled to, if the Minister decides to use the appropriate Articles of the Air Pollution Act to the full. Let me give some examples:

Every local authority must establish and maintain a register which shall be made available for inspection by the public (Article 17). However, on the content of the register, the Act is vague — "entries and additions as may be prescribed". At present this Article has not been signed by the Minister, and so it has not yet come into operation.

In Article 18, similarly, local authorities are given the **option** to publish the results of research, investigations, etc.

A pollution incident must be notified to the local authority (Article 29), but again it is up to the local authority whether or not it notifies anyone in the area who might be affected. A company applying for a licence for industrial plant *may* be asked to publish specific details. If, though, it *isn't* asked, there are obvious difficulties for those concerned who would wish to be in a position to object against a licence application, since little information will be available.

Just after our first smog alert for Dublin, which advised people to stay indoors, but did not give advice on the burning of smokeless fuel; just after the renewed initiative to set up our first municipal waste incinerator for north Dublin, where details such as the Corporation tender document as well as consultants' reports are kept as secrets, I am writing this Introduction in anger — but my anger is mixed with hope. Even with a defeat of the Freedom of Information Bill in the Senate, we will soon have as much public demand and understanding that environmental information will **have** to be produced, and reasoned public opinion taken into account. Herein, the integration of the European Community, with far reaching environmental action programmes, is providing us with a strong ally in Brussels. We do have a depressed economic situation, but we should still be able to ensure the proper management of our health and environment by taking suitable and sufficient precautions as and where they are needed.

KARIN DUBSKY
Dublin Clean Air Group.
March 1988.

SEMINAR OPENING SPEECH

ROBERT C. LEWIS-CROSBY

President, Royal Dublin Society

Welcome to the Royal Dublin Society and to its Seminar on the important subject of Air Pollution.

All through its life of over 250 years the Society has endeavoured to follow the objectives for which it was founded — namely the encouragement and improving of "Husbandry, Manufactures and other Useful Arts" — the word Sciences was added to the title at a subsequent meeting: partly I suppose because the study of science was somewhat in its infancy at the time.

As you know, the Society was instrumental in the foundation of the National Gallery, the Museum and National Library and the Botanic Gardens, responsibility for all of which was subsequently assumed by Government.

More recently the Society was concerned with the development of the National Crafts Council of Ireland. And in the Agricultural Field, and with the help of the Kellogg Foundation, three most successful Summer Schools were held in 1981, 1982 and 1983 on the subjects of energy in agricultural management, cereal production, and modern techniques in animal breeding. Summaries of their proceedings are available in Society publications. Also in the Agricultural Field a most successful seminar on cereal production was held jointly with the Irish Tillage and Land Use Society, and the Society has more recently been involved in demonstrating new methods and products in cereal production at Punchestown, Co. Kildare, in conjunction with the Farmers' Journal. These are just examples of the Society's determination to continue to carry out its purpose in continuing in the day to day activities with which you are all familiar.

Today, however, it is the turn of our Science Committee to show that one major aspect of our work has been concerned with our environment. In the early days of the Society, for example, premiums were offered for planting trees. In 1766 the Society offered premiums for the planting of weymouth pines, oak trees, scotch fir, beech, sycamore and ash trees. More recently, the Society has taken a particular interest in the Bull Island, and has published a book and a booklet on this important natural resource. Last year the Science Committee published "The Flora of Inner Dublin", by Peter Wyse Jackson and Micheline Sheehy Skeffington in cooperation with the Dublin Naturalists' Field Club. In the 1970s the Society spoke out against the proposal to site an oil refinery in Dublin Bay.

Turning more directly to the subject of air pollution in Dublin, the Society published a series of papers on atmospheric pollution in its Scientific Proceedings. One of the members of the Organising Committee of today's Seminar, Professor Denis Crowley, now a Vice President of the Society, was co-author of these reports which were produced annually from 1939 until 1943, with a further publication in 1950 referring to the years 1944 to 1950. It is therefore entirely in the tradition of the Society that the Science Committee should once again turn its attention to this environmental matter of importance, particularly since the Society is located in a part of Dublin which is particularly exposed to the problem of air pollution in our city. Air pollution is a matter of grave concern to us all whether it be in the public or private section of our daily life. Indeed, pollution of all sorts, whether of land, sea or air is of vital concern. But that is not enough. It is essential that we must all consider what must be done to counteract this problem so that future generations will not castigate us for neglect of our heritage. One has only to walk along the seafront at Sandymount or Seapoint or to look at the Bank of Ireland in College Green, whose restoration was only completed two or three years ago, to see what pollution can do to our heritage. Previous generations had their problems as well.

The holding of this Seminar is very timely in view of the fact that air pollution legislation is at present being prepared by the Department of the Environment.

What we in the Society hope is that today's lectures and discussions will result in a deeper awareness of the problem of air pollution in our city, and maybe conclusions will be reached that can be communicated to the public to accentuate the problem. Furthermore, we hope that the mood for alleviation will be greatly stimulated so as to devise means of preventing both the erosion and the destruction of our heritage.

I should like to pay tribute to the Organising Committee under the able chairmanship of Professor James Walsh for its initiative in putting this programme together. The sincere thanks of the Society are due also to the invited speakers, who are all well known experts in their areas, and we extend a particular welcome to Dr Martin Williams who visits us from England.

Finally, I should like to say a word of thanks to the commercial and industrial organisations who agreed to sponsor the Seminar. The bulk of the sponsorship will be used to publish to-day's Proceedings and, in that way, to make a more permanent contribution to the debate on air pollution in Dublin. The best thanks of the Society go to Allied Irish Banks, Bord Gais Eireann, The Coal Advisory Board, The Electricity Supply Board, Esso Ireland, The Hibernian Insurance Company, The Irish Life Assurance Company, The Irish National Insurance Company, New Dublin Gas, and the Ulster Bank.

I now finally declare this Seminar open and hand you back to our Chairman so that the proceedings can get under way. Thank you.

1

THE NATURE OF AIR POLLUTION

JAMES WALSH

Department of Chemical Engineering, University College, Dublin

Introduction

Air pollution may be considered to be the presence of adventitious substances in the atmosphere having deleterious effects on humans, animals, plants or materials.

In Dublin, the bulk of air pollution comes from the burning of fossil fuels such as petrol, oil, coal, peat and, more recently, natural gas. These fuels differ widely in their propensity to pollute.

The desirable constituents of fossil fuels are carbon and hydrogen which are combined with oxygen and nitrogen to varying degrees to form molecules of varying complexity. For example, at one end of the spectrum, natural gas is almost entirely methane whereas peat has an obviously vegetable origin with a considerable content of heavy cellulosic complexes of high molecular weight. Complete combustion of carbon and hydrogen yield carbon dioxide and water vapour, neither of which is particularly obnoxious. However, in general terms, the more complex the fuel molecule the more difficult it is to achieve complete combustion. For example, a motor car exhaust may have significant quantities of carbon monoxide, nitrogen oxides and unburnt hydrocarbons. Peat and coal can produce smoke (i.e. an agglomeration of carbon particles, dust and tarry hydrocarbons).

Incomplete combustion

Incomplete combustion is by no means inevitable, but is found to an exceptional extent in Dublin where solid fuels are burnt in the traditional form of open fire. In this respect, Dublin is unique in Western Europe and possibly in the developed world. In such circumstances as much as three per cent of the fuel may be emitted as smoke. Such incomplete combustion is not a feature of industrial type installations nor is it necessarily the case in domestic installations either. Suitable 'smoke-eater' closed stoves can be effective in reducing the smoke problem. However, to date they have had limited consumer acceptance by virtue of their initial cost and the absence of the appeal of the open fire. They also require more careful operation and more selectively graded fuel. Smokeless fuels such as anthracite and manufactured semi-cokes, and the use of natural gas, also do not present a smoke problem. Unfortunately, clean fuels tend to be much more expensive in the free market and, in times of crises, may be in short supply.

In any case it would seem more profitable today to consider how we can improve the smoke situation in Dublin at reasonable cost using available technology rather than spend our time debating whether the situation may or may not be better than at some time in the past when the situation was undoubtedly bad.

At this stage in the Seminar, the last statement may be regarded merely as an assertion. You will be the judge whether it is borne out by the material presented by the speakers who follow.

Acidity

To this point we have discussed the problem of incomplete combustion producing smoke. Incomplete combustion producing nitrogen oxides also occurs, particularly in high temperature processes such as automobile engines and gas burners, and is important not so much in its own right as in producing photo-oxident precursors to acidification, much discussed in the context of 'acid rain'.

The main source of acid in the urban atmosphere comes from the sulphur which is present in solid and liquid fuels. Coal and heavy fuel oil contain possibly one or two per cent sulphur and this burns to sulphur dioxide (SO_2). Sulphur dioxide combines directly with the moisture in the atmosphere to form relatively weak sulphurous acid. More importantly, it is photo-chemically oxidised to sulphur trioxide (SO_3) at a rate of between one half per cent and five per cent per hour and this in turn combines with moisture to form sulphuric acid, which is chemically a 'strong acid'. Such a strong acid, particularly when adsorbed on particulate matter, is potentially a hazard to human health, to plant life and to the ecosystem generally. It also attacks building materials and so increases the maintenance of our buildings and degrades our cultural heritage. Later speakers will elaborate on each of these effects.

In this paper it is appropriate to try to clarify some general ideas regarding the physico-chemical processes going on in the atmosphere. It is a truism, that can often be misleading, to say that what goes up must come down, for this begs the question as to where and in what form. For example a slow drift of air, say two m/s, will travel seven km/h and clear the city in about two hours. During that time less than ten per cent of the SO_2 will convert to SO_3 and the bulk of the acidification will take place away from the urban area at a much lower deposition intensity. However, this estimate obviously does not take into account periods of calm or the fact that some SO_2 may be 'detained' by adsorption on solid surfaces, by pools of liquid, or indeed by ingestion by individuals, so as to have all the time needed to oxidise. The international scientific community is really only coming to an understanding of such processes.

Deposition of main pollutants

Deposition of SO_x and nitrates may be wet or dry. Dry deposition involves the deposition of particles and gases by sedimentation and subsequently surface adsorption and impaction. It is more important than wet deposition close to the pollutant source but a number of details regarding it are not fully understood. Warren Spring laboratory believe that it is not possible to measure directly the dry deposition of acidity overall — one must measure the individual species. In the case of SO_2 a typical diffusion rate is eight mm/s which, for a concentration of 40 micro-g/m^3, gives a deposition rate of five g/m^2 year. If nitrous acid has been formed, it will be rapidly deposited.

Wet deposition, at distances further from the source, is largely identified with sulphate and nitrate ions and the processes of rainout and washout. The former is not as well understood as the latter.

The interpretation of data

In contrast to the more or less direct effect of smoke control technology, a more sophisticated approach is required to translate an understanding of atmospheric processes into cause-effect relationships which can be the basis of an air quality management policy. For example, is it better to devote resources to reducing SO_2 emissions or to clean up motor car exhausts? Very sophisticated modelling studies are underway elsewhere and common sense is not always a good guide. A recent feature of research has been the use of aircraft laboratories to collect data on quite a wide scale.

One could hardly advocate the expense of aircraft mounted experiments in the Dublin situation, but it is felt that more attention should be given to the mathematical modelling of Dublin pollution patterns than has been the case hitherto, and to the introduction of some more sophisticated measuring devices.

Modelling can only be done if there is appropriate basic micro-meteorological data regarding wind profiles, temperature lapse rates and inversions. This could be provided by a meteorological mast. The acquisition of such a facility by U.C.D., with the help of outside support, is under consideration, and the steps being taken in this direction could be helped by evidence of a reasonable level of informed public demand. One wonders whether a Seminar such as this has a role in such a matter?

Methods of measurement

To return to the question of monitoring, the question of instrumentation should be discussed. I pass over the pioneering work of Leonard and Crowley published by this Society around the period of the Emergency. They used deposit gauges and lead peroxide candles and the methods they used are still recognised by the appropriate British Standard No. 1747. Unfortunately it is difficult to interpret their results, valuable as they are, in terms of today's measures of pollution. For some time now, monitoring data have been collected according to parts two and three of the above standard, which in essence date from 1963/1964. Part two deals with the determination of the concentration of suspended matter by the 'standard smoke' and gravimetric methods. Only the former of these has been in use as a matter of routine. Part three deals with the determination of sulphur dioxide by wet absorption and titration and needs careful, but well understood, laboratory controls to yield reliable results. Currently the method has been partially automated to give eight day sampling. It is also referred to as the OECD Black Smoke Method.

Smoke determination depends upon drawing an air sample through a filter paper. This is then put under a reflectometer and the reading converted to a gravimetric basis using a 'standard smoke' calibration curve. Obviously, if Dublin smoke differs from the norm, say because of the presence of peat colouring, the gravimetric data will be in error. This contrasts with the direct gravimetric technique used more commonly on the Continent. Such direct gravimetric determinations have become a much more practical proposition with modern developments in instrumentation. However, it is fair to say that the black smoke method has served a very useful purpose and that calibration studies carried out in U.C.D. did not uncover any major peculiarities in regard to Dublin smoke. It seems that cost and convenience still remain valid criteria for the choice of method. Moreover, historical continuity of the pollution records is also a consideration.

There is one further point to consider in the choice of measuring technique, and this is the averaging time for the observations. The methods just described return one result per day whereas modern instrumentation using optical scatter or beta ray absorption can produce an almost continuous flow of data. In others words, such phenomena as evening peaks of pollution are smeared out by existing measuring techniques and can only be inferred from their effect upon the daily averages. In scientific terms, one would like to have as much data as possible, and the trend is in that direction. However, in terms of air quality management, it seems that the immediate need is to act on the information we already have.

A rather different problem arises from the data reduction process needed to present large amounts of information. This problem is not unique to air quality measurements. An example is that a city wide annual smoke average has little relevance in describing the situation of an individual walking between the Dublin canals on a dirty night in November. Those drafting the EEC air quality directive tried to take this into account by setting independent criteria for annual means, winter means, three day episodes, and the 98 per cent fractile. The interaction between smoke and SO_2 is also taken into account. It cannot be emphasised enough that a site does not meet the standard if it fails in any of these respects. The details of the standard will be referred to by a later speaker.

Conclusion

Air quality is a complex matter whether from the point of view of the scientist or the man in the street. Several matters of interest have not been discussed. Acid rain has recently received much attention in the context of Money Point and concern has been expressed as to the effect that development will have on the air quality throughout Ireland. One thing is sure — emissions from Money Point will have no effect upon Dublin. I personally believe it will have little effect elsewhere either and see the Money Point debate as distracting attention from Dublin where the Irish problem primarily lies. To put matters in perspective, rural winter mean concentrations of smoke and SO_2 are five to ten $\mu g/m^2$ whereas, for the overall Dublin Corporation network, smoke is in the 40-90 $\mu g/m^2$ and SO_2 is in the 40-70 $\mu g/m^2$ at some sites. Projected national SO_2 emissions even for the year 2000 A.D., when Money Point is fully operational, are less than 50 per cent up on those for 1980. A third of the people of Ireland live in Dublin. The priority for our national concern should be to deal effectively with the Dublin situation.

Another important issue is lead in the atmosphere and the introduction of lead free petrol. The latter not alone reduces lead but permits the use of catalytic afterburners on motor vehicles. Such afterburners are one method of reducing nitrogen oxides and hydrocarbon emissions. In environmental terms, such developments are to be welcomed. Currently an EEC directive, adopted in 1982, sets a limit value of two $\mu g/m^3$ for airborne lead and, after 1986, the 0.4 $\mu g/l$ lead in petrol limit set by the 1978 EEC directive will apply in this country. From October of 1985 the 1975 EEC directive limiting sulphur in gas oil to one half per cent by weight has applied here.

To close, some international comparative figures for smoke and SO_2 may be of interest (see Table 1).

Table 1: Comparative figures for smoke and SO_2

1975-76			Smoke ($\mu g/m^3$)	SO_2 ($\mu g/m^3$)
Brussels			31.8	87.2
			30.0	115.2
Amsterdam			—	44.3
			—	36.2
London			35.0	162.2
			30.9	155.0
Tokyo			54.6	69.4
			69.7	65.8
Frankfurt			58.5	107.2
			39.8	103.9
Dublin*	(Dame Street)	1975	31	91
		1976	47	86
		1978/79	44	74

WHO Offset Publication No. 41 (1978)
Dublin Corporation annual air quality reports

2

THE ATMOSPHERE AND AEROSOLS

TONY SCOTT

Department of Physics, University College, Dublin

There was a time when people thought of the atmosphere as a sponge in that it could absorb anything we cared to pour into it. Many events have changed our view on that inaccuracy but, for those of us living in Western Europe, the now famous London Smog of December 1952 brought the reality sharply into focus. And so it continues until the present with almost everyday reminders of forest trees dying, lakes being unable to support life and even buildings feeling the effects of man's outpourings of pollution into the atmosphere.

The atmosphere

It can be a worthwhile exercise to recall a few facts about the atmosphere and the way it works.

The earth's atmosphere can be thought of as a layer of gases some 80 km thick above the surface of the earth. These gases have a mass of about 5.14×10^{18} kg which result in a pressure at the earth's surface of approximately 1000 millibars. (The millibar, mb, is the unit of pressure used by meteorologists and is familiar to everyone who watches the nightly weather forecasts broadcast by almost every television station throughout the world.) About half the mass of the atmosphere lies in the lowest 5.5 km of this layer, while 98 per cent of it lies below the 30.5 km level. Above this, the density of the air is very low indeed. However, from the viewpoint of pollution, it is only the lowest 11 km that should really concern us here to-day.

If the composition of the atmosphere is examined it will be found to consist of approximately 78 per cent nitrogen, 21 per cent oxygen and the remainder of minor elements which include argon, neon, helium, hydrogen and others. One of the variable components is of course water vapour, which has many interesting and important features. Water can exist in any of three forms:— solid (ice), liquid (water) and as a vapour. When it changes from one form to another it either extracts or adds heat to the atmosphere.

The atmosphere is not static but is always in motion, either horizontally or vertically. Consider the vertical motion. In general the air ascends for at least three reasons. If air moving horizontally meets a physical barrier such as a hill or a mountain, the air must obviously rise up to pass over it. Convection is a second cause of upward movement; here warm air, being less dense, rises, while colder denser air falls. A third reason for vertical motion is due to the fact that the cold air, being denser, lies close to the surface of the earth. When a mass of air from a different region moves in, this air, if warmer, will rise up over the colder air mass.

It will be remembered that the pressure decreases with height, but of course not in a linear way. For example, if the pressure at a certain level is P then, at a point 8.4 km directly above, the pressure would be approximately P/3. The pressure continues dropping by about one third for each 8.4 km of height gained.

But consider what effect this has on a parcel of air which has ascended. This parcel now finds itself in a region of lower pressure, so it expands. This act of expansion requires

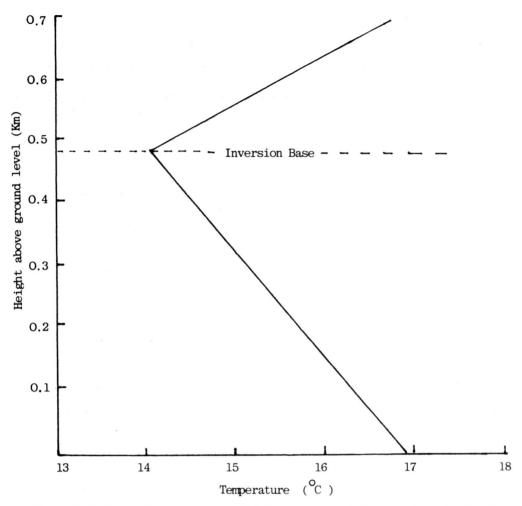

Figure 1. Variation of temperature with height below and above an inversion level.

energy and the net result is that the temperature of the air parcel drops. If the air is dry, the change of temperature with height could be about 10°C per km gain in height. But if, as is usual, there is water vapour present, then, as the air cools on ascent, condensation may occur and this process releases heat back into the parcel. The net effect will be that the variation of temperature with height — called the lapse rate — may fall to about 6°C per km.

Thus in general in the lower atmosphere the temperature falls off as indicated by the continuous line in Figure 1. However, this pattern is not always the case. It can happen that the air temperature at say the 0.6 km level may be higher than that below it (see dashed line in Figure 1). This effect is called a temperature inversion and it has an important consequence for pollution. When an inversion occurs, it prevents upward mixing and it can exacerbate a local pollution problem.

Aerosols

The atmosphere contains many particles, some of them natural but the majority, in urban areas, man made. All combustion processes release aerosols into the atmosphere.

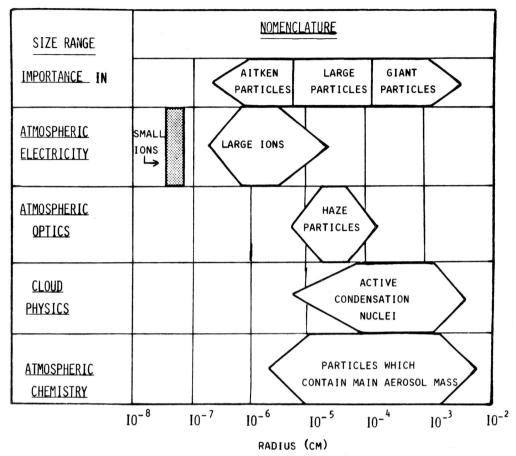

Figure 2. The role of aerosols in the atmosphere.

Thus smoke from chimneys, car exhausts and even tobacco smoke all add to the concentration of aerosols. As it can be seen from Figure 2, aerosols have a part to play in many atmospheric phenomena, but it is in the area of atmospheric chemistry that they have a role in pollution. The aerosol, if a solid, provides a surface on which trace gases can be absorbed and then react; on the other hand, if the aerosol is a liquid, the absorbed gases can react while in solution. For example, in moist conditions during a temperature inversion, sulphur dioxide from domestic or industrial sources can, in the presence of aerosols, be converted into sulphuric acid. For that reason aerosols can be used as a gauge for measuring pollution, with the observation that high aerosol concentrations are, in general, indicative of conditions of pollution.

If measurements are made on a continuous basis of aerosol concentration, some interesting features can been seen. These measurements are made using an automatic counter based on the design of Nolan and Pollak (1946). It is worth noting that Professor P.J. Nolan was awarded the Boyle Medal of the Royal Dublin Society in 1972.

Figure 3 shows measurements made at Mace Head in County Galway at a remote site away from houses. It will be noticed that the mean concentration is approximately 500 aerosol particles per cubic centimeter (cm³), while the peak value is just 1000 per cm³. In contrast, Figure 4 shows the results at the Physics Department of University College Dublin at Belfield. This site is approximately 5 km south east from the centre of Dublin

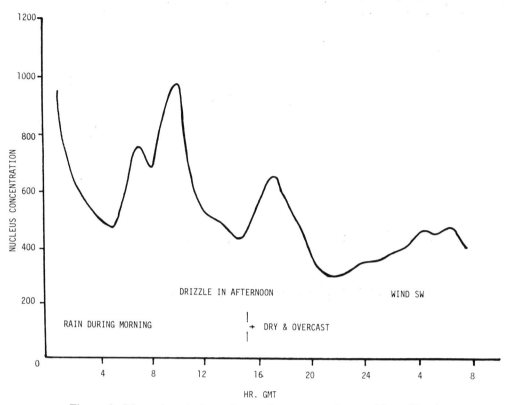

Figure 3. Diurnal variation of aersol concentration at Mace Head.

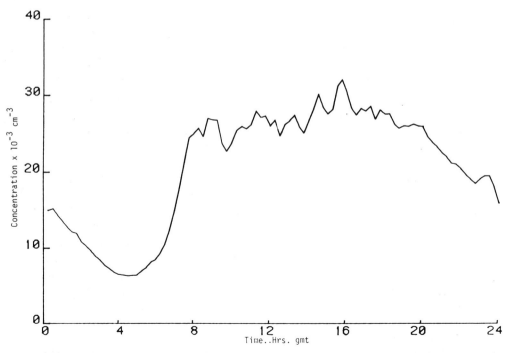

*Figure 4. Diurnal variation of aerosol concentration at Belfield in the period
August-September.*

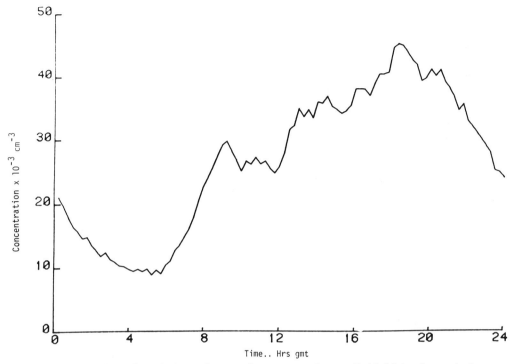

Figure 5. Diurnal variation of aerosol concentration at Belfield in the period February-March.

and is about 300 metres from a main dual carriage-way. It can be seen that the mean concentration in the period 08.00 hours to 20.00 hours is approximately 28,000 per cm³, with a peak of 31,000 per cm³. If these readings made in August and September are compared with those made in February — March (Figure 5) it will be noticed that the mean value of aerosol concentration is approximately 40,000 per cm³, with a peak of 45,000 per cm³. This represents an increase of nearly 50 per cent on the August — September values. The increase is almost certainly due to local sources not in operation in August and September, i.e. domestic fires.

Measurements were also made in the centre of Dublin with results at times going off the scale of the instrument. In general the readings were four to ten times greater than corresponding values obtained at the Belfield site.

The Papal visit to Dublin on September 29, 1979, provided a unique opportunity to examine the aerosol concentrations at the Belfield site under conditions of almost zero traffic and population movement. The traffic regulations for that day largely banned private traffic from 05.00 hours until 16.00 hours. A large car park on the campus was used by motorists who transferred to public transport for the journey to Phoenix Park. The bus movement itself largely ceased from 10.00 hours until approximately 15.00 hours. Figure 6 shows the measurements for that day. The mean concentration of aerosols in the period 10.00 to 15.00 hours was about 9,000 per cm which should be contrasted with the values for the following Saturday October 6, which are shown in Figure 7.

It is also interesting to note that measurement of the aerosol sizes shows that the mean radius in the mid-day period on September 29 was 2.15×10^{-6} cm, while those on October 6 had a mean radius of 1.32×10^{-6} cm. This can be interpreted as indicating that the aerosols on the earlier date were old, having grown by the coagulation with no

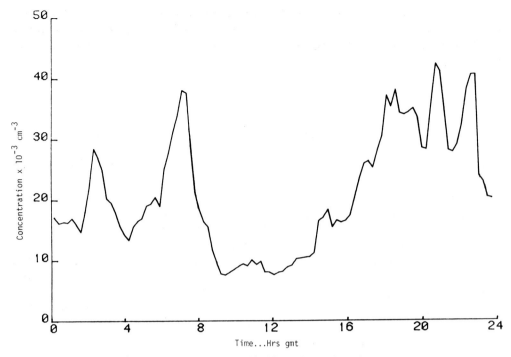

Figure 6. Aerosol concentrations at Belfield on Saturday, September 29, 1979.

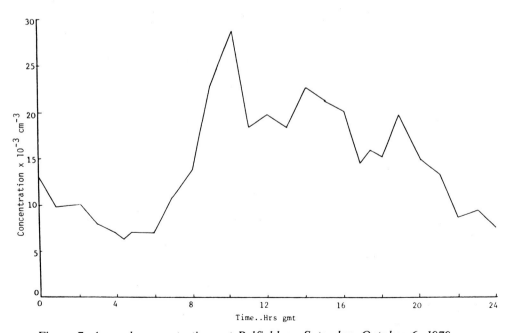

Figure 7. Aerosol concentrations at Belfield on Saturday, October 6, 1979.

new sources of aerosols being available. In general aerosols measured shortly after production by combustion are small. Thus the aerosols on October 6 are about 40 per cent smaller that those measured on September 29 due to the presence of freshly produced and hence smaller aerosols.

References

Nolan, P.J. & Pollak, L.W. The Calibration of a Photo-electric Nucleus Counter. *Proc. R. Ir. Acad.* **51 A,** 9-31, 1946.

Hayes, E.I. & Scott, J.A. An Automatic Photo-electric Condensation Nucleus Counter. *Proc. R. Ir. Acad.* **68 A,** 33-39, 1969.

Nolan, P.J. The Photo-electric Nucleus Counter — Boyle Medal Lecture. *Sci. Proc. Roy. Dubl. Soc.* Ser A **4** (12), 161-180, 1972.

Hayes, E.I. The Frequency Distribution of Atmospheric Condensation Nucleus Concentrations. *Proc. R. Ir. Acad.* **70 A,** 59-69, 1970.

Commins, K.G. *A Study of Aerosols and Ions in Urban Air.* M.Sc. Thesis N.U.I. 1980.

McMahon, G.G. & Scott, J.A. An Automatic Photo-electric Condensation Nucleus Counter with Digital Recording. *Proc. R. Ir. Acad.* **79 A,** 1979.

O'Dea, J.J. and O'Connor, T.C. Condensation Nuclei as Indicators of Air Pollution. *Irish Journal of Environmental Science* **3** (1), 32-39, 1984.

3

AIR QUALITY IN DUBLIN — THE CURRENT SITUATION

MICHAEL BAILEY

Environmental Services Section, An Foras Forbartha, Dublin 4

Introduction

Trends in air quality of a large urban area are closely related to the pattern of fuel utilisation, degree of urbanisation and type of industrialisation taking place within the area. The Dublin conurbation is expanding rapidly and, with about a million people already within an area of 290 km² (extending from Dun Laoghaire in the south, westward to Tallaght and Clondalkin, and northwards to the northern city boundary), is one of the fastest growing cities in Europe. Towards the end of the 1970s there was also a dramatic increase in the consumption of solid fuel within the domestic sector. This paper examines the associated recent trends in air quality in Dublin in relation to atmospheric emissions and concentrations. It also considers the relationship between fuel usage patterns and ambient air quality levels and what options are available to reduce urban pollution levels.

Atmospheric emissions

Emissions of smoke and sulphur dioxide (SO_2) in the Dublin urban area originate from two types of emission sources: stationary and mobile. Stationary sources include major emitters, which are usually described as point sources such as power station chimneys or area sources. This latter group comprises smaller point sources such as domestic chimneys which are treated as a single evenly distributed source. In regard to mobile sources only motor vehicles are considered important for estimating emissions in the Dublin area.

Estimates of the amount of smoke and SO_2 that may be emitted from certain fuels are shown in Table 1. It is clear that smoke emissions from coal may be 100 times or more greater than from oil.

Atmospheric emissions in the Dublin urban area

Towards the end of the last decade, the pattern of fuel utilisation changed dramatically within the Dublin urban area, particularly in regard to coal sales to the domestic sector. In 1979, as a result of the international oil crisis, there was an urgent need for this country to reduce its dependence on oil fuels. As a result, consumers were encouraged to switch to alternative fuels such as gas, electricity and solid fuel. This had a significant impact on coal sales within the domestic sector, which was enhanced by grants being offered for installation of coal burning appliances (e.g. back boilers) in domestic dwellings. The increase in atmospheric emissions arising from the change in fuel use was particularly important in relation to ambient air quality since they took place from domestic chimneys which in many parts of Dublin are only 10-15 m above ground level.

A detailed survey of fuel use within the conurbation during 1981 has been carried out by An Foras Forbartha.[1] The inventory of emissions prepared from the results of this survey was compiled on a 1 km² grid using the emission factors described above. The

Table 1: Smoke and sulphur dioxide emissions from fuels burnt in Dublin

	Fuel Type	Emissions (kg/tonne of Fuel Burnt)	
		Smoke	SO_2
Coal	Bituminous	35-50	16-20
	Anthracite	<5	20
	Processed	<5	20
Peat	Sod/Briquette	24	4
Oil	Kerosene	0.2	4
	Gas Oil	0.3	1-15[1]
	Fuel Oil	1	60-70
	Diesel	15	15[1]
	Petrol	2	1
Natural	Gas	Negligible	<0.06

[1] From October 1, 1985, emissions should not exceed 0.5% by weight. Before this date a maximum sulphur content of 0.8% by weight was permitted (EEC Directive 75/716/EEC).

Table 2: Emissions of smoke and sulphur dioxide in the Dublin urban area — 1983

Source Category	Emissions (tonnes/year)	
	Smoke	SO_2
Domestic	13,100	6,900
Commercial/Industrial	500	11,400
Power Stations	100	11,900
Motor Vehicles	2,200	1,800
Total	16,000	32,000

source categories considered were domestic, commercial, industrial, power generating and motor vehicle. In 1981, total smoke and SO_2 emissions for the area were estimated to be 15,900 tonnes and 55,400 tonnes respectively. Of the SO_2 emitted, some 35,800 (65 per cent) was estimated to have originated from the use of fuel oil at the power stations within the city. Table 2 gives the emissions of smoke and SO_2 in the Dublin urban area for 1983. It is evident that, although the estimate of the amount of emitted smoke is virtually unchanged since 1981, the emissions of SO_2 are considerably lower than the 1981 annual estimates. This is due to the fact that the Electricity Supply Board (ESB) started consuming natural gas at the main power station in Dublin and, since this fuel has a negligible sulphur content, the emissions of SO_2 therefore declined sharply.

In 1983, total emissions from all stationary and vehicle sources were estimated to be 16,000 tonnes/year and 32,000 tonnes/year for smoke and SO_2 respectively. Approximately 67 per cent of the SO_2 emitted originated from the use of fuel oil, particularly in the large industries and at the power stations (Figure 1). Sulphur dioxide emissions from coal were about 18 per cent of the total, with about nine per cent from consumption of gas oil. With regard to smoke emissions, the main source was the consumption of solid fuel, in particular coal, which accounted for 76 per cent of total emissions in the area. It is evident that smoke emissions from oil fuels are very small in comparison, with the exception of diesel driven vehicles which were calculated to contribute about ten per cent of the total in 1983.

If the fuel consumed by power stations is excluded, the total quantities of smoke produced from fuels burnt by the other source categories remain relatively unchanged; however, SO_2 emissions are reduced to 20,100 tonnes/year. Thus, for the emisson sources generally, less than about 75 metres above ground level (which include all domestic, commercial, industrial and vehicle sources), burning fuel oil contributed about 46 per cent of the total SO_2. The corresponding percentage from coal increased to 29 per cent compared to 18 per cent given above.

In regard to annual SO_2 emissions by consumer sector, the power stations, and the industrial sector, were the main emitters (Figure 2). The power stations emitted 37 per cent of the SO_2 emitted in 1983 with 22 per cent from the domestic sector and 35 per cent from the commercial/industrial sources. It should be emphasised that the 11,900 tonnes of SO_2 emitted by the power stations in Dublin are dispersed at a high level, and so the amounts originating from domestic and other low level sources will have a much greater impact on ground level concentrations. Excluding power stations, the contribution by domestic premises to the SO_2 emitted by sources generally less than 75 metres above ground, increases to 34 per cent compared to the 18 per cent value given above.

The domestic sector is the main source of smoke in the area, accounting for 82 per cent (13,100 tonnes/year) of the total. Moreover, approximately 75 per cent of these emissions are estimated to have originated from the combustion of household coal (Figure 2). An estimated 350,000 tonnes of coal were burnt in domestic premises during 1983 of which all but 10-15 per cent was household coal. Depending on how this is burnt, an estimated 30-50 kg/tonne of smoke may be produced. The remainder was comprised of

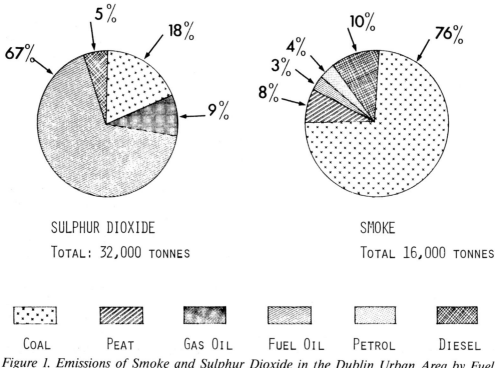

Figure 1. Emissions of Smoke and Sulphur Dioxide in the Dublin Urban Area by Fuel Type — 1983.

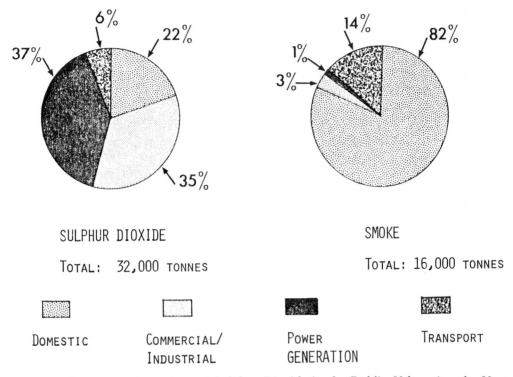

SULPHUR DIOXIDE

TOTAL: 32,000 TONNES

SMOKE

TOTAL: 16,000 TONNES

DOMESTIC | COMMERCIAL/INDUSTRIAL | POWER GENERATION | TRANSPORT

Figure 2. Emissions of Smoke and Sulphur Dioxide in the Dublin Urban Area by User Category — 1983.

smokeless fuels — either anthracite or processed fuels. Peat, small amounts of wood, and other combustible products are also burned in Dublin which can also add significantly to smoke emissions from housing estates. Road vehicle emissions contributed a further 14 per cent, most of this originating from diesel driven engines. This sector may add considerably to ambient smoke concentrations particularly in the city centre streets.

Spatial pattern of emissions in the Dublin urban area

Estimates of the distribution of SO_2 and smoke emissions on a 1 km² grid for all stationary and vehicle sources (excluding power stations) are shown in Figures 3 and 4. Although the maps relate to emissions estimated from fuel data in 1981, it is unlikely that the distribution will have changed significantly. Total emissions of SO_2 and smoke per square kilometre were estimated at about 110 tonnes/year and 55 tonnes/year respectively. There is a considerable variation in the emission rates per grid square and some areas with a high density of housing may exceed 150 tonnes/year for smoke. The pattern of emissions for SO_2 is closely related to the locations of the main industries and large commercial premises such as hospitals burning fuel oil.

A comparison may be made between Dublin SO_2 and smoke emission rates and those for the Greater London area.[2] Excluding power station sources, SO_2 and smoke emissions for London for 1978 (annual rates) were estimated to be 105,000 tonnes and 14,000 tonnes respectively. Greater London covers an area of some 1600 km² and so this gives rates per square kilometre of 66 tonnes/year for SO_2 and 9 tonnes/year for smoke emissions. Thus, annual SO_2 emission rates, averaged over the Dublin urban area, are similar to those for the Greater London area. However, annual smoke emissions per square kilometre in Dublin for 1983 were a factor of six greater than corresponding emissions for the London area. Furthermore, domestic smoke emissions in Dublin were only 1,000 tonnes lower than total smoke emissions from all sources (other than power stations) in London. It was estimated that domestic smoke emissions in 1978 within the London area were about 6,100 tonnes/year, less than 50 per cent of the 1983 value of 13,100 tonnes/year for the Dublin urban area. Motor vehicles in London now appear to be the main source of smoke (6,500 tonnes/year). The difference in smoke emissions between the two areas reflects, to a large extent, the success of clean air legislation involving designation of smokeless zones and the use of clean fuels (e.g. natural gas) in reducing smoke emissions from stationary sources in London.

Monitoring in Dublin

A network of sites for monitoring daily smoke and SO_2 levels was established by Dublin Corporation in 1973 and the site locations during 1984/85 are shown in Figure 5. There were 14 sites in 1984/85 situated within the city boundary. Two other networks have also operated in the urban area, one by the ESB and the other by Dublin County Council, but between 1979 and 1982 the data were discontinuous and hence trends are hard to interpret. During the 1970s, the ESB network consisted of 24 sites but in 1981 this was reduced to 13. It is evident from Figure 5 that there are parts of the suburbs without any monitoring sites and so are devoid of measurements on ambient pollutant concentrations. The results

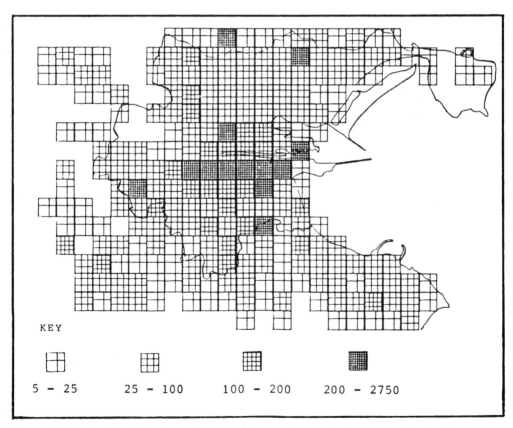

KEY

| 5 - 25 | 25 - 100 | 100 - 200 | 200 - 2750 |

Figure 3. Total SO$_2$ Emissions (in tonnes/year) from Stationary and Vehicle Sources (excluding Power Stations): 1981.

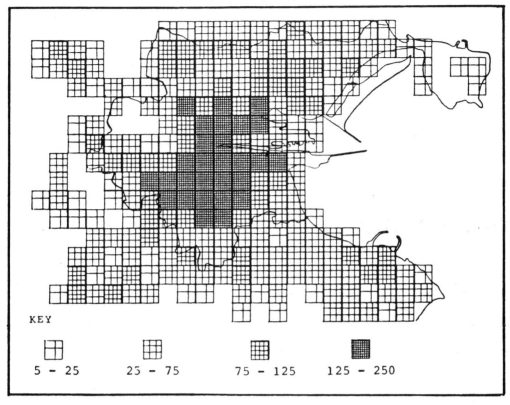

KEY

5 - 25	25 - 75	75 - 125	125 - 250

Figure 4. Total Smoke Emissions (in tonnes/year) from Stationary and Vehicle Sources (excluding Power Stations): 1981.

referred to below relate to the Dublin Corporation network, which is restricted to the County Borough area, and Dublin County Council which has five sites located on the edge of the conurbation.

The instruments and methods used are generally in agreement with OECD techniques[3] which, in turn, are based on British Standard Number 1747. The procedure used consists of passing the air sample through a filter paper to collect particulates and a solution of hydrogen peroxide to measure the acidity in the air. In an urban environment the acidity is mainly due to SO_2. It should be mentioned that the smoke concentration depends on the darkness of the filter paper stain. For example, diesel smoke gives a blacker stain than that from ordinary domestic smoke. Both pollutants are expressed as $\mu g/m^3$.

EEC Air Quality Directive

In 1980, an EEC Directive on air quality limit values and guide values for SO_2 and suspended particulates[4] was adopted. Its provisions became mandatory on April 1, 1983. It specifies limit values for annual, winter and daily periods for both SO_2 and suspended particulates (interpreted as smoke in relation to monitoring in Ireland). In the case of SO_2 limit values, account is taken of the possible synergistic effect of the two pollutants occurring together. The daily limit values should not be exceeded for more than three consecutive days, though seven daily exceedences are permitted during a given year (Table 3). The Directive also specifies that plans for improvement of air quality and procedures

Table 3: The 1980 EEC Air Quality Directive Limit Values for SO_2 and Smoke ($\mu g/m^3$)

Reference Period	Limit Value for SO_2	Associated Value for Smoke	Absolute Limit Value for Smoke
Year	80	< 40	80
(Median of Daily Means)	120	≤ 40	
Winter	130	< 60	130
(Median of Daily Means October-March)	180	≤ 60	
Day	250*	<150	250*
(98 percentile of daily means values)	350*	≤150	

*Member States must take all appropriate steps to ensure that this value is not exceeded for more than three consecutive days. (Source: Council Directive 80/779/EEC.)

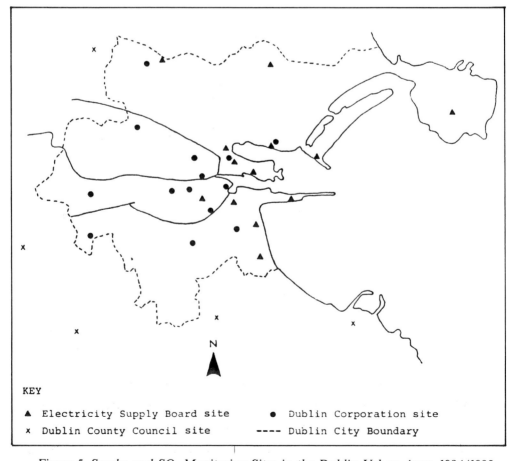

Figure 5. Smoke and SO$_2$ Monitoring Sites in the Dublin Urban Area: 1984/1985.

must bring the concentrations of the two pollutants to values below or equal to the limit values by April 1, 1993, at the latest.

Dublin air quality

Results from the Corporation network indicate that between 1973 and 1981 there was an overall decline in SO_2 levels, and to a lesser extent smoke. Average winter concentrations of SO_2 decreased from 101 $\mu g/m^3$ to 54 $\mu g/m^3$ during this period. Smoke levels similarly declined from a winter average of 62 $\mu g/m^3$ in 1973/74 to 34 $\mu g/m^3$ by 1980/81 (Figure 6).

During the period 1981/82, however, this overall improvement in air quality was arrested when several days were observed with very high levels of air pollutants, in particular smoke. This was primarily due to a number of occasions when climatic conditions over Dublin prevented rapid dispersion of pollutants from low level emission sources. The average winter smoke level for the whole network increased by about a factor of two in 1981/82 to 90 $\mu g/m^3$ and was 50 per cent higher than any preceding winter since the present network was established. Moreover, for the first time, the average smoke level for the network exceeded that for SO_2. With regard to SO_2, the ambient concentrations were comparable with those observed in the mid-1970s, reaching a network

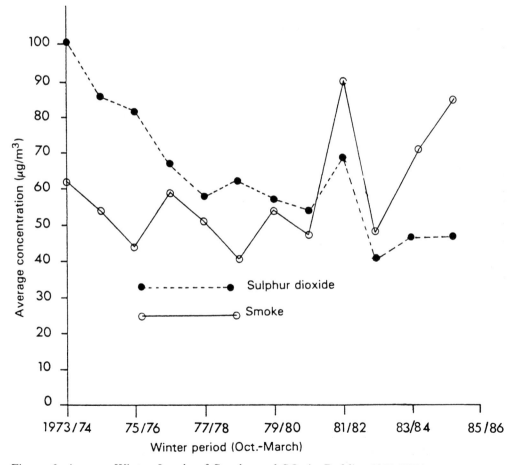

Figure 6. Average Winter Levels of Smoke and SO$_2$ in Dublin: 1973/1974 — 1984/1985 (based on results of the Dublin Corporation Network).

winter average of 68 $\mu g/m^3$. The deterioration in air quality during 1981/82 is evident when the average levels at each site are examined. For example, four sites had a winter average smoke level in excess of 100 $\mu g/m^3$ and, from the results, it is apparent that the deterioration was widespread.

Ambient smoke and SO_2 declined in 1982/83, but it should be emphasised that this was the predominance of unsettled weather for much of the winter rather than a decline in emissions, thus preventing any air pollution episodes.

In 1983/84 and 1984/85, however, the average winter smoke concentrations increased once again to 71 and 86 $\mu g/m^3$ respectively. Although these levels are not as high as in 1981/82, the deterioration in air quality in terms of smoke levels compared to that observed during the late 1970s, is clearly evident. Sulphur dioxide ambient concentrations were significantly lower, with a winter average of 46 $\mu g/m^3$ for both winter periods, which is less than the ambient levels recorded during the 1970s (Figure 6).

In regard to ambient levels recorded by Dublin County Council, smoke concentrations have recently increased at each of the sites compared to those observed in the late 1970s. Although the levels are considerably lower than those recorded by city centre sites, the incidence of days with levels greater than 200 $\mu g/m^3$ has increased. The winter mean smoke levels at all the sites are significantly greater than for SO_2, once again reflecting the predominance of smoke as the main pollutant.

An evaluation of results from the Dublin Corporation monitoring sites in the light of the 1980 EEC Air Quality Directive limit values is given in Table 4 for the annual periods 1973/74 — 1984/85. The sites that would have breached the limit values, if they had been in effect, during the mid-1970s were due primarily to the high SO_2 levels being recorded. During 1981/82 a total of eight of the 13 operational sites would have exceeded the daily limit values for smoke. Two city centre sites also exceeded the annual limit value for SO_2. In 1983/84 five sites exceeded the daily limit values for smoke and one site failed to comply with the winter median limit value for smoke. This was also the first winter since 1974/75 that a site had exceeded the winter median limit value.

Table 4 also shows that the number of daily site observations greater than 250 $\mu g/m^3$ increased to 145 in 1981/82 and 125 in 1984/85 compared with previous years. The maximum daily smoke concentration at any site since the network was established was recorded during a particularly severe air pollution episode in January 1982. Very high smoke levels (in excess of 1000 $\mu g/m^3$) were observed at some sites during an air pollution episode from January 11-15 1982, when an intense ground based inversion and low temperatures (minimum daily average $-3.2°C$) were recorded. The daily average smoke level for the whole network from January 11-14 was in excess of 300 $\mu g/m^3$. Levels of SO_2 were much lower, with a maximum daily concentration of 418 $\mu g/m^3$ measured at one of the city centre sites.

This episode is a good example of how under calm, very cold, anticyclonic conditions, pollutant levels can quickly become very high. Although such severe meteorological conditions are infrequent, even during 1983/84 and 1984/85 there were several pollution episodes resulting from low level inversions.

Even though the maximum concentrations of 795 $\mu g/m^3$ were much lower than observed in 1981/82, there were more incidents of relatively high smoke levels. During the 1983/84 and 1984/85 winters, smoke levels in excess of 250$\mu g/m^3$ were observed at one or more sites on 45 and 38 days respectively compared to 31 in the 1981/82 winter.

The greater incidence of air pollution episodes in Dublin in recent years demonstrates clearly how air quality can quickly deteriorate given certain weather conditions. Under anticyclonic conditions the wind speed will be very low and, as a result of strong radiation cooling of the ground towards evening, a low level temperature inversion can quickly

Table 4: Number of Dublin Corporation sites exceeding the EEC Directive Limit Values and the number of site observations greater than 250 $\mu g/m^3$ of smoke

			Limit Values		
			Daily		No. of daily Smoke Observations >250 $\mu g/m^3$
Period	Annual	Winter	98% of daily mean values	More than 3 consecutive days	
1973/74	4*	—	4*	2*	28
1974/75	2*	1*	3*	1*	6
1975/76	2*	—	1*	1*	—
1976/77	—	—	1*	2+	35
1977/78	—	—	1+	1+	33
1978/79	—	—	—	—	4
1979/80	—	—	1+	—	39
1980/81	—	—	—	—	8
1981/82	2*	—	7+	7+	145
1982/83	—	—	—	—	27
1983/84	—	1+	5+	1+	101
1984/85	—	—	6+	4+	125

Note: Numbers of Sites with value data: 12 for 1973/74 to 1979/80; 13 for 1980/81 to 1981/82 and 14 for 1982/83 to 1984/85.
  *indicates SO_2 value; +indicates smoke value.

develop. With the increased quantities of smoke being emitted from low level sources, these pollutants can become trapped close to the ground causing a rapid increase in pollution levels. The episode in 1982 mentioned above took place under extreme meteorological conditions and provided the first indications of how high pollution levels may rise under certain climatic conditions. However, the results of 1983/84 and 1984/85 indicate that smoke levels can increase quickly under less severe weather conditions. Therefore, the present pattern of air quality in Dublin is dependent primarily on meteorological factors rather than emission trends.

Air quality and energy policy in Dublin

A change in fuel use can have important implications for the air quality within an urban area. For example, a rapid increase in the use of a highly polluting fuel (e.g. coal) or the introduction of a clean fuel (e.g. natural gas) can have a significant effect on the air quality of the area. The magnitude of this impact will depend not only on the penetration by the new fuel into the existing energy supply market, but also on the consumer sector, such as domestic or industrial, in which the penetration takes place. The contribution of the emission source category to present ground level ambient air quality will determine how effective the change in fuel use will be at reducing levels of air pollution.

The emission height is of particular importance in assessing the relative contribution of different source categories to ambient ground level concentrations. Thus, it is the relatively low level sources e.g. domestic, commercial, industrial and motor vehicle, that will have the greatest impact on ground level concentrations in an urban area.

The fuel change options available for improving the air quality depend on the relative costs of certain fuels, fuel availability and the costs involved in changing from one fuel to another.

Conclusions

The importance of low level emission sources, particularly the domestic sector, in contributing to the ambient air quality of the Dublin urban area has been clearly demonstrated during recent winters. Unless there are widespread changes in fuel use within the domestic sector towards cleaner fuels, or installation of smoke-reducing combustion appliances, then smoke emissions in Dublin will remain relatively unchanged from present levels. At present, high pollution levels are occasionally reached at certain sites in Dublin, especially when climatic conditions prevent rapid dispersal of emissions. These high levels have on a number of occasions exceeded international standards designed to protect human health. The Air Pollution Act is a particularly welcome piece of legislation and should be fully used to bring about an improvement in the air quality in the area. However, extensive monitoring and development of air pollution models are also important to enable areas where control measures are required to be identified and the success of these measures assessed.

Acknowledgements

The author wishes to thank the Atmospheric Pollution and Noise Control Unit of Dublin Corporation who provided the monitoring data on which this paper is based.

References

1. Bailey, M.L. *Air Quality in Ireland — Recent Trends in Atmospheric Emissions and Concentrations.* A report prepared for the NBST by An Foras Forbartha, Dublin. WR/C85, 1983.
2. Schwar, M.J. and Ball D.J. *Thirty Years On — A Review of Air Pollution in London,* Greater London Council, 1983.
3. OECD. *Methods of Measuring Air Pollution,* OECD Publications, Paris, 1964.
4. Council of the European Communities. *Council Directive on Air Quality Limit Values and Guide Values for Sulphur Dioxide and Suspended Particulates,* 80/779/EEC, Brussels, 1980.

4

AIR POLLUTION — HEALTH IMPLICATIONS

GEOFFREY DEAN

The Medico-Social Research Board
(Now, The Health Research Board)

Introduction

As a medical student in Liverpool before the war I would frequently see on the ground in the centre of the city blobs of thick yellow greenish sputum and, in the hospital medical wards, there would be a line of middle-aged men coughing thick spit into their tin sputum mugs which they had on top of their lockers. The city buildings were black with grime from the city smoke and the lungs of our patients at autopsy were as black as the buildings. The factories and domestic chimneys poured forth smoke so that in the evenings visibility was so bad it was not possible in winter to see across the River Mersey. Smog often made driving very difficult so that, on occasions, it was necessary for someone to walk ahead of the car at night with a torch so that the driver could find his way home.

During the war it was the policy in Britain to produce as much smoke from the factories as possible in London and central England as this made it very difficult for raiding German planes to bomb accurately. This was a good example of what was considered to be an "acceptable risk"; the risk of accurate bombing was considered to be greater than the risk of increased respiratory illness that might result from heavy atmospheric pollution.

There had long been pea soup fogs in London, well described in Victorian times in the Sherlock Holmes stories but, after the war, in 1952/53, during severe winter smog, there was such an increase in deaths from respiratory disease that Parliament was forced to take drastic action and introduce the Clean Air Act (1956)[1] forbidding the use of domestic coal in smoke-free zones and strictly controlling the emission of smoke from factory chimneys. About this time, Doll and Hill in England, and Hammond and Horn in the United States, showed the very strong statistical relationship between the number of cigarettes smoked and the risk of dying from lung cancer and other respiratory diseases.[2,3]

South Africa

In 1947 I emigrated as a ship's doctor from Liverpool to South Africa and was surprised to find that, although the white South Africans smoked on average more cigarettes than the British at home, immigrants to South Africa from the United Kingdom, aged 45-64, had higher lung cancer rates than the white South Africans.[4] This was evidence that there was a British factor, over and above cigarette smoking, that was responsible for lung cancer, probably the result of bronchial damage from air pollution.[5] Most British immigrants came to South Africa from cities and at a relatively young age. Eastcott in New Zealand[6] and Haenszel in the United States[7] also found that the British immigrants to those countries, where there was a high cigarette consumption, had higher rates of lung cancer than the native-born and I found it was also true in Australia.[8] Chronic bronchitis was so common in Britain that it was often called the British disease on the Continent. It is uncommon in South Africa.

Table 1: South Africa: The "British factor" — lung cancer — white male lung cancer mortality 1947-56. Rates per 100,000 (Source — Reference 5).

Age	45-49	50-54	55-59	60-64	Total 45-64
Johannesburg:					
Union-born	19	70	130	180	72
British immigrants	(48)	115	101	233	117
Other	(33)	49	111	139	75
Cape Town:					
Union-born	36	95	79	141	76
British immigrants	(55)	(93)	228	222	145
Other	(31)	(23)	(51)	(145)	56
Durban:					
Union-born	50	78	199	229	111
British immigrants	(44)	139	286	259	178
Other	(47)	(46)	(139)	(242)	114
Pretoria:					
Union-born	(26)	74	113	127	71
British immigrants	(55)	(52)	(195)	(201)	118
Other	(56)	(71)	(0)	(50)	(45)
Port Elizabeth:					
Union-born	(13)	(65)	(65)	(124)	53
British immigrants	(43)	(142)	(203)	(130)	125
Other	(0)	(64)	(0)	(0)	(20)
Other urban areas:					
Union-born	15	43	55	115	48
British immigrants	45	58	93	95	71
Other	(14)	(28)	100	170	68
Rural areas:					
Union-born	10	19	38	62	30
British immigrants	(0)	(79)	(22)	285	94
Other	(0)	(18)	(59)	(109)	(38)
Total:					
Union-born	17	45	63	103	50
British immigrants	44	91	144	187	112
Other	25	38	89	149	67
Total:	20	49	75	120	58

Males lung cancer deaths 1947-56. England and Wales

Age	45-	50-	55-	60-	Total 45-64
Rate per 100,000	57	116	185	233	135

If the numbers are below 10, the rate is in brackets.

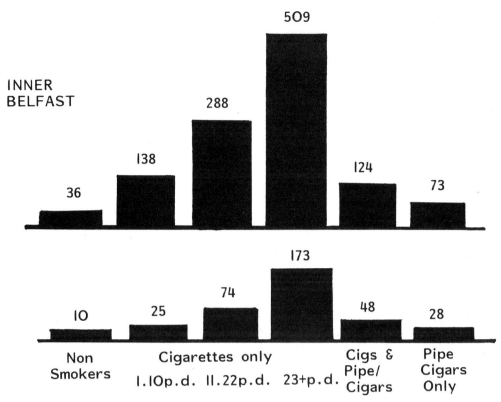

Figure 1. Northern Ireland lung cancer mortality rates of men in inner Belfast and the truly rural districts — per 100,000 per year, age standardised, 1960-1962, among men aged 35+ (Source — Reference 9).

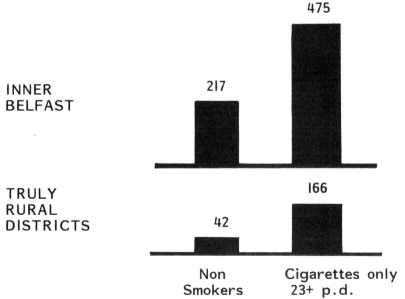

Figure 2. Northern Ireland bronchitis mortality rates of men in inner Belfast and the truly rural districts — per 100,000 per year, age standardised, 1960-1962, among men aged 35+ (Source — Reference 9).

In the 1950s, it was becoming clear that both lung cancer and chronic bronchitis are associated with both city air pollution and cigarette smoking. Cigarette smoking is the more important factor in lung cancer and, in chronic bronchitis, both urban air pollution and cigarette smoking play a part.

Northern Ireland

In 1963 I was asked to undertake a study of mortality from lung cancer and chronic bronchitis in Northern Ireland and found that both in Belfast and in the rural areas the risk of dying from lung cancer was directly proportionate to the number of cigarettes smoked. For each level of smoking, however, even for non-smokers, the risk of dying from lung cancer was about three times greater in inner Belfast than it was in the rural areas. On the other hand, the heavy smoker had 17-20 times the risk of lung cancer as the non-smoker. Deaths from chronic bronchitis were strongly associated with living in Belfast.[9]

The Republic of Ireland

In 1968 I was invited to become the first director of the Medico-Social Research Board of Ireland. Among the first projects undertaken by the Board were studies on the causes of death in the Republic of Ireland. We found death rates were higher in Dublin than in the rural areas of the Republic. This was particularly true of respiratory disease and of heart attacks. In Dublin people smoked more and more people smoked than in the rural areas but, as in Northern Ireland, there appeared to be an urban factor associated with respiratory disease besides the cigarette smoking factor.[10]

In 1976, the Board undertook a study on behalf of the EEC on respiratory disease in schoolchildren, aged 7-11, in Dublin, Cork and Galway and found that children who grew up in homes where the parents smoked had more respiratory disease than those with parents who were non-smokers. Air pollution was worse in Dublin and in Dublin there were more respiratory symptoms in the children.[11]

During the past few years it has been Government policy to build houses with coal-burning fireplaces and Dublin has had an increasing amount of air pollution from domestic fires and from factories. There is also the increasing air pollution that occurs from the great increase in the number of motor cars. We have not yet removed lead, a potentially dangerous pollutant, from our petrol, we say for economic reasons, although this has been done by EEC directive in the other countries of the Community.

The 1984 report by An Foras Forbartha, *Air Quality in Ireland. The Present Position*[12] pointed out that there had been a 30% increase in smoke emissions between 1975 and 1982. The rise was most pronounced following the dramatic increase in the use of coal in 1979 as a result of the 1979 oil crisis. Annual sulphur dioxide (SO_2) emission levels, averaged over the Dublin urban area, are comparable to those of Greater London and smoke emissions, similarly averaged, are six times higher than in the London area.

Sulphur dioxide and smoke emission in the Dublin area are monitored by the Electricity Supply Board and by Dublin County Council. During the winter of 1981/82, eight of the 13 operational sites exceeded the EEC daily limit value for smoke, and two sites exceeded the annual limit for SO_2.

Fortunately, it is unlikely that Ireland experiences significant acid deposition from sources in Europe as the prevailing wind is westerly, but our SO_2, no doubt, blows across the Irish sea and a coal-burning power station in Co. Clare may increase the SO_2 in the air over Ireland unless we are prepared to pay the cost of installing scrubbers to remove the smoke particles and SO_2.

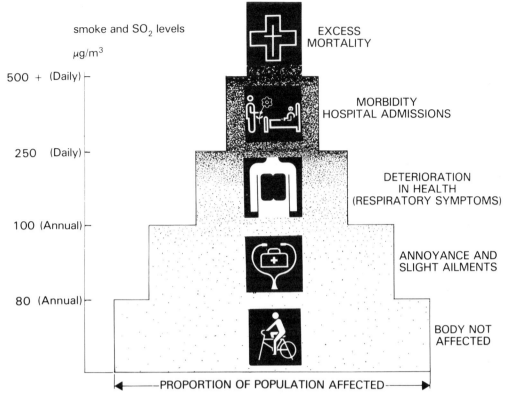

smoke and SO$_2$ levels
μg/m^3

500 + (Daily)
250 (Daily)
100 (Annual)
80 (Annual)

EXCESS MORTALITY

MORBIDITY HOSPITAL ADMISSIONS

DETERIORATION IN HEALTH (RESPIRATORY SYMPTOMS)

ANNOYANCE AND SLIGHT AILMENTS

BODY NOT AFFECTED

◄——PROPORTION OF POPULATION AFFECTED——►

Figure 3. Expected Health Effects of Smoke and SO$_2$ and spectrum of biological response — based on World Health Organisation criteria (Source — Reference 12).

Conclusion

There is no doubt that the most harmful form of air pollution is cigarette smoking and, while to smoke or not to smoke is a personal decision, it should certainly be public policy that nobody should smoke to pollute the air of their neighbours in public buildings or on public transport.

There is very good evidence that urban air pollution not only damages human health but also damages the environment — in the city, buildings, and in the country, trees and vegetation, by the production of acid rain. There is an old Lancashire adage "Where there's muck there's brass" and there is no doubt that the strict control of air pollution costs money. The decision to what extent we will control our air pollution and pay the necessary costs is a political one and includes the concept of "acceptable risk". Do we accept a high level of air pollution and the harmful effects it produces on health and the environment in order to keep more people in employment and maintain their standard of living?

If we are to reduce air pollution, which undoubtedly affects health, decisions are required at two levels; the personal decision not to smoke and the public decision, depending on public opinion, that we will pay the cost, as has now been done in London and many other cities of Britain and of Europe, of restricting pollution of the atmosphere from factories, domestic fires and transport. There is a cost to pay and whether or not we will pay it is for the public to decide.

Table 2: Republic of Ireland — Urban-Rural Differences 1970-72   (Source — Reference 10).

ICD Code	Cause	Dublin County Borough			Remaining Urban districts			Rural districts		
		Actual Total	Expected Total	SMR	Actual Total	Expected Total	SMR	Actual Total	Expected Total	SMR
	MALES									
B5	Tuberculosis of respiratory system	84	52.1	161	75	62.0	120	203	248.0	82
B19c	Malignant neoplasms of trachea, bronchus and lung.	653	322.5	202	526	388.0	136	1112	1580.4	70
B28	Ischaemic heart disease	2229	1934.0	115	2631	2410.3	109	9858	10373.5	95
B33	Bronchitis, emphysema and asthma	769	490.8	157	816	614.8	133	2177	2656.5	82
	FEMALES									
B19c	Malignant neoplasms of trachea, bronchus and lung	187	132.3	141	168	144.5	116	337	415.2	81
B33	Bronchitis, emphysema and asthma	442	343.5	129	418	382.6	109	979	1112.7	88

The "Expected total" is calculated from the all Republic of Ireland rate.
SMR = Standardised mortality ratio.

References

1. Clean Air Act, HMSO, London, 1956.
2. Doll R. and Hill A.B. A study of the aetiology of carcinoma of the lung. *British Medical Journal,* No. 2, 1271, 1952.
3. Hammond E.C. and Horn D. Smoking and death rates — Report on 44 months of follow-up of 187,783 men. *Journal of the American Medical Association.* Parts I and II, 1159, 1294, 1958.
4. Dean G. Lung cancer among white South Africans. *British Medical Journal,* No. 2, 852, 1959.
5. Dean G. Lung cancer among white South Africans. *British Medical Journal,* No. 2, 1599, 1961.
6. Eastcott D.F. Epidemiology of lung cancer in New Zealand. *Lancet,* 1, 37, 1956.
7. Haenszel W. Cancer mortality among the foreign-born in the United States. *Journal of the National Cancer Institute,* 26, 37, 1961.
8. Dean G. Lung cancer in Australia. *The Medical Journal of Australia.* 1, 103, 1962.
9. Dean G. Lung cancer and bronchitis in Northern Ireland, 1960-2. *British Medical Journal,* No. 1, 1506, 1966.
10. Ward J.B., Healy C. and Dean G. Urban and rural mortality in the Republic of Ireland. *Journal of the Irish Medical Association.* 71, 3, 73, 1978.
11. *EEC epidemiological survey on the relationship between air pollution and respiratory health in primary school children.* Report of the Commission of the European Communities, 1984.
12. Bailey M.L. *Air quality in Ireland. The present position.* An Foras Forbartha, Dublin, 1984.

5

AIR POLLUTION DAMAGE TO DUBLIN'S HISTORIC BUILDINGS

DAVID JEFFREY

Department of Botany, Trinity College, Dublin

Introduction

This is a preliminary account of one part of a co-operative and interdisciplinary study funded by the EEC. The participants are the Director of Buildings and Environmental Sciences Unit, TCD, the School of Architecture, UCD, and the Office of Public Works. We believe that the interagency-interdisciplinary approach to this problem is fundamentally important and partly explains our success in coming to grips with it quickly. Nevertheless, some explanation is required of my own involvement as a plant ecologist. The connection is very simple. First, the process of soil formation by rock weathering, and the availability of ions to plants, entail the same chemical mechanisms as stone damage. Secondly, the ecological approach requires measuring simple responses to a frequently very complex environment. Design of experiments and analysis of data in ecology can contribute to materials testing under field conditions. Thirdly, the use of very sensitive chemical analytical techniques, in particular atomic absorption spectroscopy, is well established in ecosystem studies. For example, ecologists have been studying for decades the chemistry of waters running off tree trunks and interpreting their composition *vis à vis* bulk rainfall.

Lastly, the study of responses of plants to air pollutants is a very active field at the present time. There are two clear aspects to this field: a) the study of fumigation by gaseous pollutants, in particular sulphur dioxide (SO_2), oxides of nitrogen (NO_x) and ozone (O_3); b) the responses to acid rain.

Fumigation studies have yielded a whole series of dose-response relationships, but a very clear message is the importance of synergism. This means that the combined effect of two pollutants, especially SO_2 and NO_x, is much greater than the sum of their parts.

The acid rain story is more complex, with the recognition of biological effects going back for about 100 years to the worst excesses of the industrial revolution in Lancashire. When hydrogen ions fall on a catchment, the biological consequences will vary according to the soil pH, cation exchange capacity, base saturation and general geochemistry. If the soil pH falls towards pH 5, the hydrogen ions (H^+) start to attack the crystal lattice of alumino silicate minerals releasing trivalent aluminium (Al^{+++}) into soil solution. At concentrations of a few parts per million, Al^{+++} can have direct inhibitory effects on a) root metabolism, causing root death in some species: pathogen attack may also be encouraged, increasing vulnerability to drought, b) microbial processes, especially key links in nutrient cycles such as nitrification rate.

Any affected catchments will become sources of Al^{+++} ions to the whole of the watershed. Wildlife of lakes and water courses will be adversely affected either directly by Al^{+++} or indirectly by flocs of aluminium hydroxide. Such flocs may have a clogging effect on gills of small invertebrates and larger fish.

The stonework of historic buildings

Although there is a large literature describing the ravages of the atmosphere on stone buildings and monuments, we know less about the chemical mechanisms than we do of effects on vegetation. One of the aims of our research programme is to provide some insight into the relationship between rate of damage and urban environmental conditions.

In Dublin it must be appreciated that damage has already occurred. The eroded face of the National Museum, the cleaned and refurbished facade of the Bank of Ireland, and more recently of the Custom House, are well known examples of damage and its repair. In Trinity College, the balustrades crowning the 18th century buildings of Front Square have recently been replaced. The balusters had become so weakened by erosion that their structural integrity was seriously threatened. We can say that Dublin faces a multimillion pound restoration task.

The questions are: 'just how serious is the current rate of damage?' 'Is it wise or futile to clean, protect or restore historic buildings?' 'What, in pollution terms, needs doing about abatement?' Putting this last question the other way round, 'What causes stone decay?'

Three materials call out for examination, Portland Stone, Leinster Granite, and Copper, which are incorporated into most of our historic buildings, and many modern ones for that matter.

The chemistry of the weathering of these materials is set out in Figure 1.

A number of conclusions may be drawn from this rather commonplace chemistry:

i) The hydrogen ion is an important common ingredient.

ii) Single elements, as their ions, may be used as indices of weathering, viz

Calcium (Ca^{++}) from Portland Stone
Potassium (K^+) from Granite
Copper (Cu^{++}) from Copper Sheet.

The microcatchment unit

From the above questions, it was deduced that we required an experimental module to study short term weathering effects on building materials in the urban environment.

We have now developed and built a series of what we term "microcatchment units" (Figure 2). A microcatchment is a piece of selected material 625 cm^2 (about 1 foot square) fitted to act as a small watershed, and provided with a means for collecting runoff. This simple concept has required careful development to ensure that runoff water is not lost or contaminated. Further studies have led to a mounting system which ensures that the thermal performance of our modules is closely similar to materials incorporated into buildings. Furthermore, it has been established that the Ca^{++}, K^+ and Cu^{++} ions released can be readily measured in the runoff water. Analysis of rainfall must also be undertaken to establish by difference exactly what is removed from the stone or copper sheet. We can now claim a world first in achieving a scientifically valid measure of stone decay measured weekly!

Environmental monitoring

There are many environmental effects which contribute to stone decay. These are summarised in Table 1. It is important to realise that freeze thaw cycles and thermal expansion-contraction alone can damage surfaces. We are probably studying these physical processes with a set of chemical reactions superimposed. In particular the transport of acidity is important. There are at least four ways in which stone surfaces can be exposed to acid:

limestone – Portland stone

$$CaCO_3 + 2H^+ \longrightarrow Ca^{++} + CO_2 + H_2O$$

$$CaCO_3 + H_2SO_4 \longrightarrow CaSO_4 + CO_2 + H_2O$$

gypsum

granite

feldspars + quartz & mica

weathering   released as crystals

$$2KAlSi_3O_8 + 2H^+ + H_2O \longrightarrow$$

feldspar

$$Al_2Si_2O_5(OH)_4 + 4SiO_2 + 2K$$

kaolinite   silicate   potassium

powdery   soluble

clay mineral

copper sheet

$$2Cu + 2H_2SO_4 + O_2 \longrightarrow 2CuSO_4 + 2H_2O$$

soluble
copper sulphate

but

green patina $Cu_4(OH)_6SO_4$

brochanite

stained stonework $CuCO_3.Cu(OH)_2$

Figure 1. The conventional chemical equations for weathering are not simple or necessarily well understood.

a) Acid rainfall, in which dilute acids, formed by oxidation of SO_2 and NO_x, add to the natural carbonic acid of rainfall. This may be explored by careful analysis of rainfall pH supported by N and SO_4 determinations. It leads to erosion of exposed surfaces.

b) Direct fumigation with acid forming gases which may react with moist stone surfaces.

c) Associated with particulates, especially soot. The blackened surfaces of buildings, usually rather protected by building details from direct rainfall, indicate the importance of particulates. Whenever this black crust is examined it is comprised of Gypsum (Figure 1) with embedded soot particles. The stone beneath is frequently very porous and decayed. Soot is seen as a possible carrier of acids.

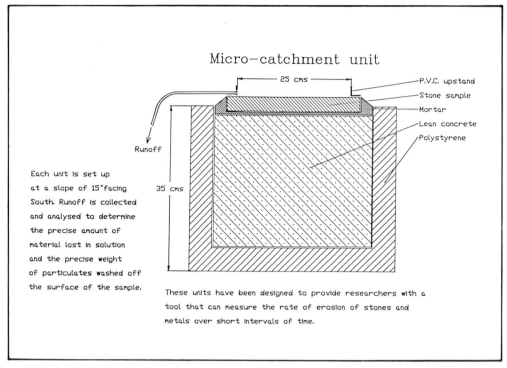

Figure 2. The final form of the microcatchment unit.

Table 1. Environmental effects which contribute to stone decay.

Rainfall	i) General statistics of bulk precipitation. ii) Rainfall events — storms vs drizzle. iii) Rainfall chemistry — see below.
Relative Humidity	See dewpoint excursions.

Temperature	i) Surface temperature of stone surface.
	ii) Temperature gradients — thermal stress.
	iii) Temperature excursions
	   (a) freeze thaw cycles
	   (b) dewpoint excursions — condensation when a surface temperature is less than dewpoint for a particular relative humidity.

Pollutants	i) Acidic gases SO_2 and NO_x
	ii) Rainfall chemistry H^+, NO_3, SO_4, Cl [Ca, K, Cu]
	iii) Particulates
	   (a) solid — estimated as smoke particles
	   (b) aerosols and condensate

Transport of acidity	a) Rainfall — erosion of exposed surfaces b) Associated with particulates $\}$ c) As aerosols or condensate $\}$ Damage to exposed and "protected" surfaces.

d) Associated with aerosols or condensate. Recent studies on the acidity of catchments have shown that the bulk precipitation, as trapped in a raingauge, seldom accounts for all acidity received. The remainder is associated with so called 'occult' precipitation as mist or dew. These slow forming droplets of moisture may have a greater capacity to absorb and oxidise acid forming gases.

Thus there are possible explanations for attack of both exposed and protected surfaces.

The Dublin experiment

We have now set up two experimental arrays in Dublin. One is in the heart of the city on the roof of the northern pavilion of Regent House, TCD. This overlooks College Green and Westmoreland Street. The site is literally surrounded by the buildings we are trying to protect. The other is on the roof of the School of Architecture, UCD, at Richview, Clonskeagh Road.

At each site we have microcatchments with old and new Portland Stone, Granite, and Copper, each being studied in duplicate.

At both sites we have measurements of SO_2, smoke, rainfall, relative humidity, and rainfall chemistry. Temperature of surfaces and interiors of units is being measured using 16 channel recorders. Thus temperature gradients may be determined, and compared with the surfaces of the actual buildings.

Results

It is too early to start talking in detail about results for a pair of reasons. First, we have barely a full season of records available at the present time. Secondly, as must be apparent from the description of the experiment, the environmental data generated are very complex. A computer data base is being compiled and we will need help from both statisticians and mathematicians to give a final interpretation.

However, it is worth presenting some samples. The loss of Ca^{++} from old and new Portland Stone surfaces for a 12 week period in spring 1985 is shown in Figure 3. Taking the regression lines for this short period at their face value, it is seen that the more porous old surface, carefully removed from a TCD balustrade, is weathering more quickly than the new stone. In fact, about one gm of Ca is being removed from a square meter a week in the TCD site. Translating this into dimensional terms is not easy, because each portion of dissolved calcium releases a bit more as a particulate grain of $CaCO_3$. A very rough conservative approximation would give a surface recession rate of between 0.7 and 1.0 cm of surface per century. This is not acceptable, being about twice the rate of the last 200 years and at least 100 times faster than rates for an unpolluted situation.

To illustrate the nature of the data processing problem, Ca loss is presented with but two environmental measurements, SO_2 and rainfall (Figure 4). For this late summer period, rainfall and Ca loss are closely related. Although the SO_2 readings are increasing as the days shorten, the rainfall values declined over this period. This indicates that some effects may be delayed as our measurement system depends closely on rainfall. We will be inspecting data closely for larger or smaller ion removal than can be accounted for by the current rainfall. This may entail applying time series analysis to the data, as well as more conventional statistics.

As a last example, I would like to mention an understanding of a very characteristic Dublin phenomenon which we have achieved. Frequently, Portland Stone is used in detailing on granite faced buildings. Close inspection of the granite shows a faster weathering rate close to the ornamentation. Furthermore, this is very well marked on the

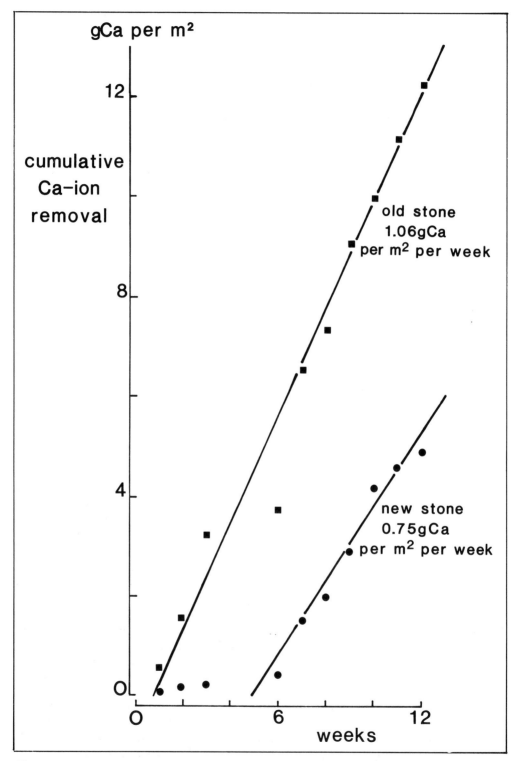

Figure 3. Some preliminary results of 12 weeks weathering of old and new Portland Stone, 25.3.85-17.6.85. A simple linear regression analysis is applied to the cumulative calcium ion removal data to calculate rates of weathering.

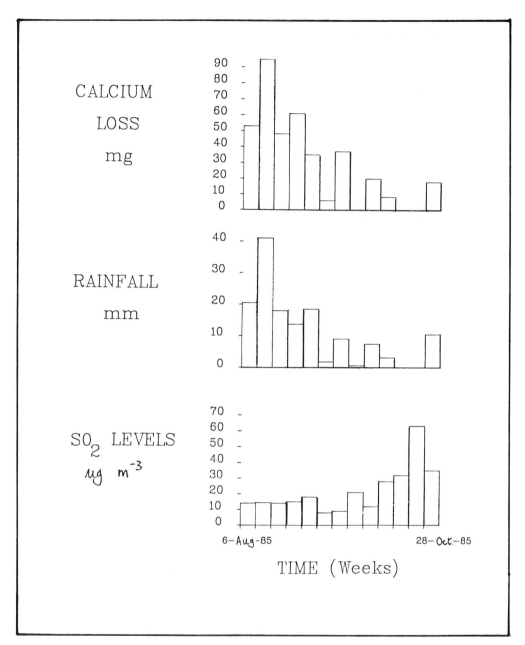

Figure 4. Two environmental variables, rainfall and SO₂, are seen in context of weekly Ca removal from Portland Stone. This illustrates the difficult data analysis problems to be solved.

southfacing sides of buildings. A good example is the Museum Building, TCD, which houses the Department of Geology. We suspected that gypsum formation could be at the heart of this problem, because the formation of gypsum crystals, as solution wetted surfaces dry, is known to generate physical forces. The Geology Department duly examined a series of granite specimens for us using X-ray diffraction spectrometry. Gypsum crystals were associated with the decayed granite. Thus the scheme for accelerated granite decay appears to be as presented in Figure 5. This finding has already been applied to a practical

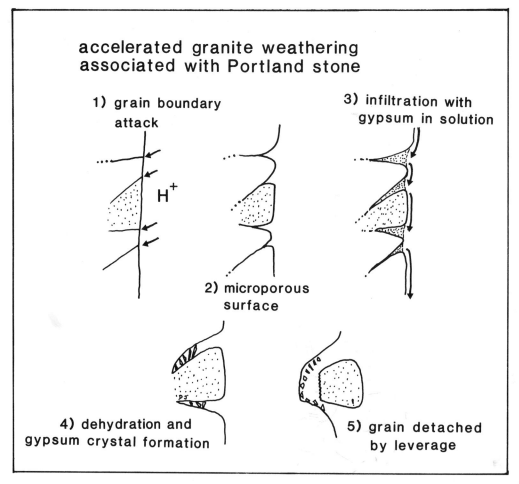

Figure 5. Schematic reconstruction of the effect of Portland Stone or lime mortar on granite weathering.

task, the repointing of the Dining Hall, TCD, currently being refurbished after the fire in 1984. A low calcium mortar has been specially developed to avoid the further accelerated decay of the granite facing. The calcareous building sands of Dublin, when incorporated into mortar, have the same effect as Portland Stone.

Future developments

It is particularly gratifying to report an Irish development in materials testing, which has a bearing on materials protection and pollution abatement. We would like to set up a European microcatchment network in order to get results into a wider perspective. Another development is the testing of treatments for stone and metal surfaces, with design work already started. The system seems to be adaptable to many modern building materials, including composites. Some modern buildings are even more vulnerable to soiling and damage from polluted air.

Knowing the rate of damage will assist in establishing some cost of depreciation values attributable to pollutants. This scale of values can be directly interfaced with fuel use economics, especially when combined with the rather well established costs of mortality and morbidity resulting from air pollution developed by the OECD.

Although we are concentrating on the fabric of historic buildings, and in particular three materials, there is a large field waiting to be explored and explained.

In many 18th century buildings, iron clamps were used to support stone-work. Delicate structures such as steeples were invariably built with iron reinforcement. These have deteriorated, giving very expensive repair tasks, as stones have frequently been split by accumulating rust.

In modern materials, concrete and galvanised roof sheeting deteriorate more rapidly in urban sites. To the urban and suburban householder the replacement of curtains and the painting of woodwork are tangible added costs.

Acknowledgements

In presenting this paper, I gratefully acknowledge the contributions of the whole study team: Tim Cooper, Director of Buildings, TCD; Paul O'Brien, Environmental Sciences Unit, TCD; J. Owen Lewis and Geraldine O'Daley, School of Architecture, UCD; and David Slattery, Office of Public Works.

X-ray diffraction studies on granite were carried out by Dr David Doff, Geochemistry Laboratory, TCD.

This project is funded under the 3rd Environmental Research Programme of the EEC, Contract No. *ENV. 871 EIR.*

Further reading

G. Amoroso and V. Fassina. *Stone Decay and Conservation,* Elsevier, New York, 1983.
T.H. Mansfield. *The effects of air pollution on plants,* Cambridge University Press, Cambridge, 1976.

6

TECHNICAL POSSIBILITIES FOR ALLEVIATION

MARTIN REILLY

*Atmospheric Environment Department, Institute for Industrial Research and Standards
(Now, EOLAS)*

Introduction

The only possible solution to this problem of meeting the EEC Directive on air pollution (see page 25), as I see it, is to stop the burning of coal, peat and wood in domestic households. The exact mechanism as to how this might be achieved I do not propose to go into in this paper. It is covered in the Air Pollution Act of 1987. The mechanism adopted in the UK to achieve this will be described in the next paper.

Such a situation will affect most of the households in Dublin. Over 60 per cent of households in Dublin use coal as their main form of heating either from an open fire with or without a back boiler for water heating for washing purposes or with a back boiler for partial central heating by radiators. Of the remaining 40 per cent, many of these use an open fire for occasional heating.

Many of us in Dublin seem to have a sentimental attachment to an open fire but it should not be forgotten that this is the most inefficient form of heating. The efficiency of an open fire is at best 25 per cent. This means that only a quarter of the potential heat in the coal is supplied to the room being heated, with the other three-quarters going up the chimney. A back boiler will only at its very best double this efficiency up to 50 per cent when the boiler surfaces are clean, but the average efficiency in use will only be about 40 per cent.

I shall now consider the options available to householders involving change over to a cleaner fuel — natural gas — or a cleaner form of heating — electricity — or smokeless solid fuels. The costs of the various fuels are given in Table 1.

Natural gas option

The natural gas pipeline to Dublin was completed in 1982 and Dublin Gas are in the middle of a conversion programme to change from manufactured town gas to natural gas. Over 60 per cent of households in Dublin are connected to the gas main although this is primarily for cooking with only about ten per cent of households using gas for heating. Most of the other households in Dublin, certainly within the Dublin Corporation area, are accessible to the gas mains. The present gas reserves in the Kinsale Field are sufficient for at least 20 years even with a major switch to natural gas for heating, and it would be surprising if further gas fields were not found in the area. The mains network of Dublin Gas is capable of supplying all the demand for heating.

The cost of a gas fired room heater can be anything from £100 for a basic model upwards to £1,000. The cost of heating a room of 20m² to a comfortable level from early morning to 11 p.m. at night for the 6 months heating season using a gas fired room heater would be £300 for the year (£240 if gas also used for cooking, £210 if gas used for cooking and water heating). The cost of running an open fire in the same room to give the same

Table 1: Domestic Fuel Costs — Dublin Area 1 July 1985

Fuel	Unit	Cost £	Cost (p/kWh)[2]
Dublin Gas	therm	[1] 1.44 for first 16	4.91
		1.09 for first 24	3.72
		0.79 for remainder	2.70
		or	
		0.88/therm minimum of 550 therms/annum	3.00
Liquid Fuels			
Gas Oil	litre	0.3038	2.88
Kerosene	litre	0.3029	3.01
LPG (Propane)	11 kg cyl.	8.55	5.65
Solid Fuels			
Anthracite (Grade A)	tonne	217.55	2.41
Anthracite (Blend)	tonne	182.05	2.28
Extracite	tonne	210.06	2.47
Household Coal	tonne	137.41	1.65
Peat	25 kg bag	4.03	1.93
Peat Briquettes	bale	1.05	1.63
Electricity			
General Domestic[3]	kWhr	0.0785	7.85
Urban Economy[4]			
Night (11pm-8am)	kWhr	0.0380	3.80
Day (8am-11pm)	kWhr	0.0785	7.85

[1]This tariff relates to a 2 month billing period.
A standing charge of £4.00 per 2 months applies.
[2]The cost figures relate to fuel as burnt and do not take into account appliance efficiencies.
[3]A basic standing charge of £3.00 for 2 months applies.
[4]An additional standing charge of £6.00 per 2 months applies.

standard of heating using coal would be £385. The savings made would pay for the average cost gas fire in a short period of time.

Dublin Gas are currently quoting £899 for the installation of a gas fired room heater with back boiler. The annual running cost of such a system in a three bedroom terraced house maintaining a comfortable level in the house would amount to £350. The annual cost of running an open fire using coal in the same house to give the same level of heating would be £435.

From this it can be seen that it would take a long time to pay back the cost of such a conversion and it can hardly be justified on economic grounds. It does, however, have other advantages such as convenience and less maintenance and cleaning.

Electricity

Electricity is a clean fuel in its use. It should not be forgotten that there are emissions of sulphur dioxide and other pollutants in its generation at the power station. At present approximately 15 per cent of households in Dublin City use electricity as their main form of heating. Many of these appear to use direct electrical appliances rarther than storage heaters.

The cost of an electric storage heater plus a direct electrical heater would be of the order of £250. The running cost of such an appliance on the night rate with a topping up with a direct heater on the day rate as required for a 20m^2 room heated to a comfortable level as before would be £245 per annum. If a direct electrical appliance were used for the same duty on the general domestic rate the annual cost would be £355. These compare with the cost of an open fire using coal to give the same duty at £385 per annum. This makes both options cost effective with the storage heater having a quick pay-back period.

More extensive heating by storage heaters would not be cost effective as compared to an open fire with a high output back boiler. For a three bedroom terraced house at least six storage heaters would be required. These would cost approximately £1,200. The running cost would be £420 as compared to £435 for an open coal fire with high output back boiler.

Smokeless solid fuels

There are several smokeless solid fuels available both naturally occurring and manufactured. The most familiar smokeless solid fuel is the naturally occurring anthracite. There are considerable reserves of this in Ireland but there appear to be economic difficulties in mining it. It is not suitable, however, for use in open fires and can only be used in closed appliances. Open fires with and without back boilers can be converted to closed fires by the use of the Waterford Ironfounders Firedoor. The cost of these is of the order of £200. This will improve the efficiency of the open fire and, while the cost of anthracite is about 50 per cent greater than coal, the running cost will be considerably less than that of an open coal fire.

Taking the case of heating a 20m^2 room to a comfortable level, the annual running cost with the fire front and burning anthracite will be of the order of £225 as compared to £385 for an open coal fire. This will pay for the cost of the installation in a very short period of time. In the case of a fire with a high output back boiler, the running cost in the case of a 3 bedroomed terraced house will be £425 with the fire front fitted and running on anthracite as compared to £435 for an open coal fire.

There are some manufactured smokeless solid fuels which are suitable for use in open fires. The only adaptions these would require are possibly a stronger grate such as a "firemaster" which cost about £30. The most well known of these manufactured fuels is Coalite. This is not generally available in Ireland but could be imported from the UK where supplies are plentiful again since the end of the Miners' strike.

It is likely to cost about 50 per cent more than coal but this is more than made up for by its greater efficiency and heat output even on an open fire. The net result is that the running cost would be much the same as for coal. There may be a tendency initially for people to pile this up on their fire in the same way as they did for coal so that the cost would be higher at first until people got used to the greater heat output.

District heating schemes

There is no doubt that District Heating Schemes are cost-effective, certainly for new housing estates, but they do also have significant environmental benefits. They have not been used in Ireland mainly because of difficulties with the control of heating in the Ballymun scheme and the need to set up an administrative system to run the scheme. However, they are very common in continental Europe and are widely used on new housing estates in the UK.

In these the heat is raised at a central boiler house and piped to all the houses in the scheme. At the boiler house the fuel used is usually coal but a wide variety of fuels can be used — even domestic refuse. At the boiler house efficient controls can be installed to reduce smoke emissions and a sufficiently high stack can be installed to effectively disperse the sulphur dioxide and other pollutants.

Other possibilities

There are several appliances on the market which will burn coal smokelessly. These have been approved for use in smokeless zones in the UK. All of them are closed appliances and hence their efficiency is much greater than that of an open fire—typically of the order of 60 per cent. The cost of these is in the range £500-£700 depending on installation requirements.

Coal Distributors Ltd have developed an open fire for burning coal with an inbuilt afterburner which will reduce smoke emissions by the order of 50 per cent. This is intended to fit into existing fireplaces at a reasonable cost.

Conclusions

1. The only solution to the problem of meeting the EEC smoke and sulphur dioxide directive by 1993 is to prohibit the use of coal, peat and wood in domestic fires.
2. There are plenty of alternative options available to householders involving change of fuel to gas or electricity or the use of smokeless solid fuel, most of which are more efficient and less costly to run than the inefficient open coal fire.

7

THE UK EXPERIENCE

MARTIN WILLIAMS

Warren Spring Laboratory, Stevenage, UK

Introduction

This paper will attempt to provide a very brief overview of the developments in air pollution in the UK over the last forty years or so. A discussion of trends in the emissions of major air pollutants will be given together with associated air quality measurements. The bulk of the discussion will be concerned with smoke and sulphur dioxide (SO_2), since there is much more information available, in terms of both emissions and air quality, for these pollutants, and because air quality legislation in a domestic UK and European context has been primarily concerned with these species.

However, some discussion of measurements of other pollutants such as nitrogen oxides (NO_x), ozone and acid deposition will also be given.

Smoke and sulphur dioxide

These pollutants have attracted the most attention over the past 40 years or more in the UK and it is only for these pollutants that air quality data on a detailed national scale exist in the UK. Similarly the national emissions of SO_2 are probably the best documented and most accurately known.[1] The first EEC air quality directive to be promulgated addressed these pollutants,[2] and it is these species which formed the subject of much health effect work in post-war UK[3] during the period when "smogs" were occurring in major cities in the UK. This section will briefly review the history of emissions and air quality data for smoke and SO_2, particularly in the context of the framework of the management of air quality in the UK.

Emissions

In considering the emissions of SO_2, two timescales will be considered. Firstly from the early 1900s to the present, and secondly during the period from 1960 to the present day.

Considering the longer period first, the increases in industrial activity and living standards during the twentieth century have led to an increase in fuel consumption and hence SO_2 emissions as shown in Figure 1. Sulphur dioxide emissions increased from a figure of about 2.5-3 million tonnes in 1900 to a peak of 6.09 million tonnes in 1970. The recent trend is shown in more detail in Figure 2 where a broad disaggregation by source type is shown. From this graph it can be seen that, following the peak year of 1970, UK SO_2 emissions have decreased by about 42 per cent to a 1984 total of 3.54 million tonnes. This recent decline has taken place chiefly in the low and medium level source sector (domestic, commercial/public sector, small/medium industry) and has arisen broadly equally from a combination of factors — general energy conservation measures, increased penetration of North Sea Oil (of relatively low sulphur content), industrial modernisation and a change in fuel use patterns, in both the domestic sector and in the industrial/commercial sector, towards fuels of lower sulphur content.

The pattern of this recent decrease in terms of broad source categories has important consequences for air quality as will be seen in the following section, since at locations

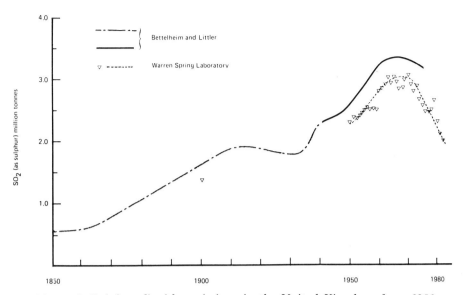

Figure 1. Sulphur dioxide emissions in the United Kingdom from 1850.

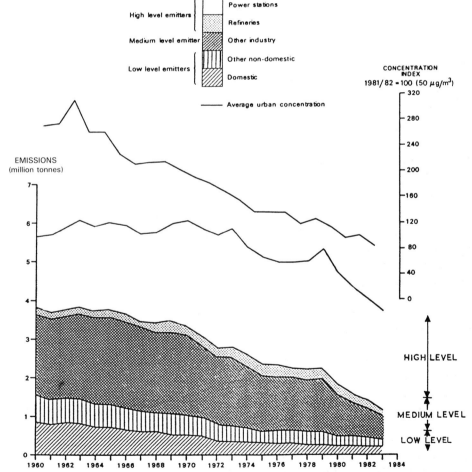

Figure 2. Sulphur dioxide: emissions from fuel combustion and average urban concentrations in UK.

remote (greater than say 30-50 km) from source regions, the height of emissions is relatively unimportant and airborne concentrations are determined chiefly by total emissions, while low and medium level emissions have a much greater proportional impact in the near field (within 0-10 km say).

Emissions of smoke are less accurately known than those of SO_2 chiefly since smoke emission factors must be measured for each fuel and user type while, to a very good approximation, SO_2 emissions can be calculated from the fuel consumption and sulphur content of the fuel concerned. Smoke emissions have historically largely arisen from coal combustion and it is for this fuel that emissions have been estimated. The situation is complicated by the difficulty of relating mass emissions of particulates (on a gravimetric basis) to measured concentrations of "black smoke" which are not strictly in gravimetric units. The mass emissions of particulates from coal combustion in the UK from 1960 to the present are shown in Figure 3. In the late 1960s, coal combustion accounted for about 70 per cent of all smoke emissions. The emissions have decreased dramatically over this period, primarily due to the decline in domestic coal consumption.

It is appropriate at this point in our discussion of historical trends in emissions to discuss briefly the legislative developments in air pollution control policy which were occurring in the UK.

As long ago as 1906, with the Alkali etc Works Regulation Act, the UK began to exercise control over "noxious or offensive gases" from certain industrial works. With this Act and with the subsequent Health and Safety at Work etc Act of 1974 and the associated Health and Safety (Emissions into the Atmosphere) Regulations 1983, the control of emissions from registrable works (including power stations, cement works, iron and steel etc) is exercised by the Industrial Air Pollution Inspectorate.

In terms of the reduction in domestic coal consumption and emissions, the principal legislation enforced by local authorities (LAs) in Great Britain is contained in the Clean Air Acts of 1956 and 1968 which allowed LAs to make Smoke Control Orders. The more recent Department of Environment (DoE) Circular 11/81 removed the requirement to refer proposals to the Secretary of State.

The increasing extent of smoke control in the UK is shown in Figure 4 where the cumulative acreage and premises under smoke control orders are plotted together with domestic coal consumption. The strong correlation between the increase in smoke control and decrease in domestic coal consumption might suggest a stronger causal link than was actually the case. It is very probable that, despite the onset of smoke control, a certain fraction of the population would have moved away from the use of coal to the more convenient oil and gas fuels. Nonetheless it is reasonable to conclude that this implementation of smoke control programmes throughout the UK has been the major cause of the reduction in domestic coal consumption over the past twenty or so years. The high correlation between domestic coal consumption and smoke concentrations over this period is indeed the result of a causal relationship, particularly in the earlier part of the period, although, where concentrations have decreased to relatively low levels in recent years, the proportionate contribution from other sources, notably motor vehicles, will now of course be larger.

There are now over 5,800 smoke control orders operating in the UK covering over 800,000 hectares and almost two-thirds of urban properties. Exchequer backed local authority grants are available to householders for any necessary conversion work, total costs being split between Central Government, local authorities and owners in the average ratio 40: 30: 30. Expenditure on such work rose steadily during the 1960s to a peak of over £7m in 1973/4 but since then has declined to £3.2m in 1983/4. This to some extent reflects the fact that the worst areas have now been tackled.

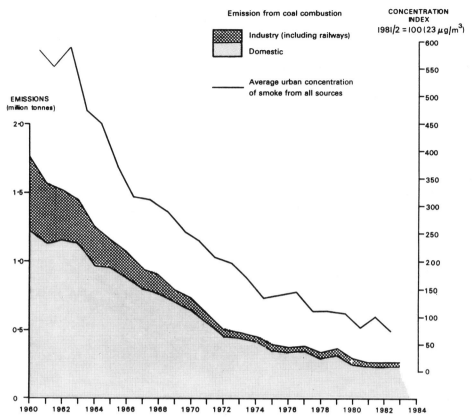

Figure 3. Smoke: emissions from coal combustion and average urban concentrations in UK.

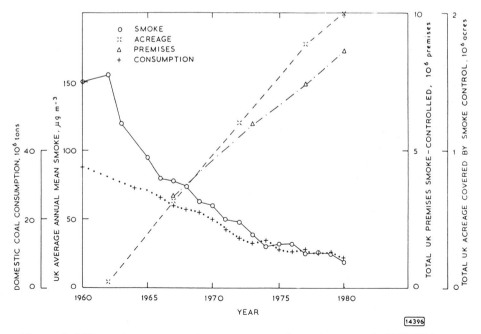

Figure 4. UK smoke concentrations vs extent of smoke control, 1960-1980.

Air quality

As has already been mentioned, the changes in emissions of smoke and SO_2 have had important consequences for air quality in the UK. Turning first to SO_2, the decrease in emissions in the past 15 years or so has been primarily from low and medium level sources. This important fact, together with to a lesser extent the move away from smaller power stations in or near urban areas to larger plants in more rural areas, has resulted in significant decreases in urban concentrations of SO_2. The national average of urban SO_2 annual mean concentrations is shown together with the emissions data in Figure 2, from which the close relationship between low/medium level emissions and air quality is clear. Average urban concentrations have fallen by about 70 per cent since 1962. A plot of SO_2 concentrations at two sites in the City of London is shown in Figure 5.

The decrease in smoke concentrations over the same period is even more pronounced as can be seen from Figure 3, where average urban concentrations have decreased by almost an order of magnitude since 1960, and the "smogs" which affected London and other major cities in the UK have now been eliminated.

It is interesting to analyse the historical smoke and SO_2 data before the marked reduction in coal consumption, in terms of the EEC Directive limit values. In view of the reasonably uniform downward trend of both smoke and SO_2 concentrations (as UK averages) since 1960, the analysis has not been carried out for every year but only for a sufficient number of years to indicate the general trend, and the results are shown in Figure 6.

The height of each column measures the total number of sites in the UK which breached any of the EEC Directive limit values for the particular pollution year beginning in April of the year shown on the x axis. It can be seen from the figure that the total number of sites breaching the limit values has fallen broadly in line with the decrease in smoke concentrations. In 1962/63, for example, the number of sites breaching was 925 which was 98 per cent of all the sites with data, while in 1979/80 the number was 58 or six per cent of all sites. The relationship between the frequency distributions of UK sites and the ratio of the 98th percentile to median limit values in the Directive is such that, for the UK sites, the 98th percentile limit values are in general the more stringent. To demonstrate this, particularly in relation to the importance of smoke concentrations in determining breaches of the limit values, the data have been analysed to identify the number of sites which breach the 98th percentile limit value for smoke alone, i.e. regardless of the corresponding SO_2 concentration. This value is 213 μgm^{-3} in terms of the British Standard calibration curve as used in the UK. The numbers of such sites are also shown in Figure 6 from which it is clear that in the early 1960s the breaches of the limit values were due almost entirely to elevated smoke concentrations. In the mid- to late 1960s and in the 1970s coal consumption and hence low level smoke emissions declined. So, too, did low and medium level SO_2 emissions, and the total number of breaches of the limit values declined. During this period, the fraction of total breaches due entirely to elevated smoke concentrations (i.e. those sites with annual 98th percentiles of smoke > 213 μgm^{-3}) also declined and the fraction due to other causes increased. Most of these other breaches (about 20 per cent of all breaches to 1979/80), shown by the shaded sections in Figure 6, occur because the 98th percentile "smoke trigger" value of 129 μgm^{-3} is exceeded so that the more stringent SO_2 limit value applies.

Notwithstanding this trend, it is clear from Figure 6 that, where breaches occur, the extension of smoke control with a reduction in low level smoke emissions is likely to be the most effective way of ensuring compliance with the limit values in the UK. Although not presented here, a more detailed analysis reveals that the majority of sites remaining

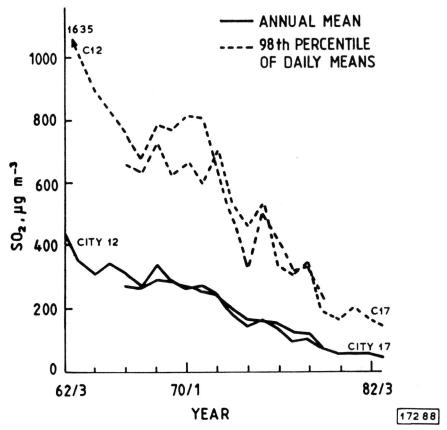

Figure 5. SO₂ trend data — sites near St. Paul's Cathedral.

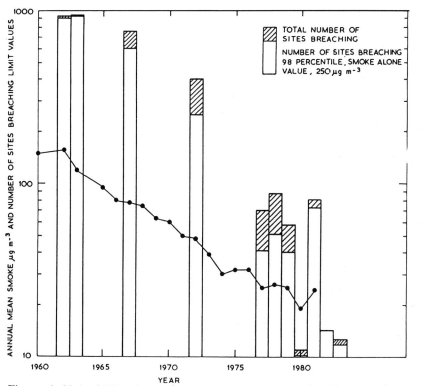

Figure 6. United Kingdom annual network averages for black smoke.

in breach in the period since 1977 are in areas of relatively high coal consumption and where, overall, smoke control is not yet complete.

Dispersion modelling studies

In view of the foregoing discussion and analysis of emissions and air quality, it is almost self-evident that, in the late 1950s and early 1960s, the dominant source of smoke and SO_2 in urban areas was domestic coal consumption, so that a dispersion modelling study of that period may be considered, prima facie, to be of questionable value. However, it is instructive to consider the results of such an exercise carried out some years ago by Warren Spring Laboratory (WSL),[4] in order to attempt to quantify the proportional source contributions from the domestic and other sectors. There is insufficient space in this paper to describe the calculation in detail; a Gaussian plume-type model was applied to the London smog episode of December 1962 and to a period in December 1975 when smoke and SO_2 concentrations were higher than had been observed for some years. Although the emission estimates were relatively crude, and the fact that a Gaussian model in such low wind speed episodes is not a good approximation, the results give a reasonable picture of relative source contributions. In the 1962 episode, the contribution of domestic coal combustion to smoke concentrations was up to 70 per cent (already smokeless fuel/coke had begun to be used in significant quantities in the domestic sector in London — 1.7 million tonnes in 1962 — and contributed 20 per cent to smoke concentrations). The contributions of both domestic coal and coke to SO_2 concentrations in the 1962 episode was 25 per cent (giving 50 per cent from the domestic sector in total). By 1975 the relative contributions to smoke concentrations had decreased to 20 per cent from domestic coal and 25 per cent from smokeless fuels; the corresponding contributions to SO_2 concentrations being five per cent and 20 per cent respectively. Current relative contributions from the domestic sector will be even lower and probably amount to about five to ten per cent to both smoke and SO_2 concentrations in winter periods.

In the present context, it is perhaps useful to compare these estimates with similar ones for Dublin. Emissions data for Dublin have recently become available,[5] and a recent modelling study[6] concluded that the domestic sector was responsible for about 65-70 per cent of the annual average smoke concentrations in Dublin in 1978. Of this domestic contribution, on average about 75 per cent arose from coal combustion. More recent emissions data[7] suggest that these proportional contributions have not changed significantly in the intervening period.

The discussion thus far has centred on the relative contributions from source categories. The important quantity, however, is the absolute values of the smoke and SO_2 concentrations. It is not the intention of this paper to address this issue for Ireland, which has been adequately covered elsewhere in the seminar. The absolute smoke concentrations in Dublin are currently considerably lower than those observed in London during the mid to late 1960s where, during high pollution episodes, daily mean values of the order of about 2-4000 μgm^{-3} were observed. However, in terms of *proportional* contributions to smoke concentrations, the current situation in Dublin is similar to that in London in the mid-1960s, when domestic coal was making a contribution of 70 per cent to ambient smoke concentrations.

Other pollutants

Nitrogen Oxides (NO_x)

There are considerably fewer measurements of NO_x (NO and NO_2) available than for smoke and SO_2 in the UK. WSL has operated a series of sites over the past ten years or so, and a summary of the results at one of the sites with the longest runs of data is shown in Figure 7. The contrast with the previous trend data for smoke and SO_2 is revealing. Estimates of national emissions of NO_x in the UK[1] suggest that roughly 40 per cent arise from motor vehicles and a similar amount from power stations. Emission factors for NO_x are less accurately known than are those for SO_2 for example, but, even allowing for these uncertainties, there is no marked trend in NO_x emissions in the UK over the last 15 years or so and the air quality data which exist broadly reflect this. Over a longer timescale, however, estimates suggest that UK emissions of NO_x have increased quite significantly since 1946 (see Figure 8). There is some evidence from aerosol nitrate data in the period 1957-1980 that these emission changes are to some extent reflected in the nitrate concentrations.[8] However, a more detailed analysis of the relationship between NO_x emissions and air quality data would require longer runs of ambient NO_x concentrations at more sites than currently exist, and improved estimates of NO_x emission factors and emissions.

Ozone

There has been interest in ozone as a pollutant for many years in both North America (where ozone is one of the Environmental Protection Agency's criteria pollutants for which a health-related air quality standard exists) and in Europe. In recent years interest in ozone has further increased due to observations that crops may suffer damage from ozone concentrations and that the gas may be a contributing factor to the reported tree damage in Germany. WSL has measured ozone at several sites in the UK over the past ten years or so and a summary of some data at Sibton is shown in Figure 9.

There is currently considerable interest in Europe in investigating strategies for the control of ozone concentrations by reducing emissions of the precursor pollutants NO_x and the reactive hydrocarbons which, under the action of sunlight, form ozone and other so called "photochemical" pollutants on a range of timescales. While the broad principles of ozone formation in the atmosphere are well understood, the ozone forming potential of particular source areas can be sensitive to the relative proportions of NO_x and hydrocarbons in the emissions and to the proportions of the individual reactive hydrocarbons. The efficacy of a given set of controls on precursor emissions in reducing ozone concentrations can therefore vary from one source region to another and, for a given source region, can vary at different down-wind distances. This means that, before attempting to impose controls on precursor emissions to reduce ozone concentrations, a thorough modelling investigation of the photochemistry of the region in terms of the relative proportions of precursor emissions is essential, otherwise costly controls can be imposed with the possibility that little or no reduction in ozone concentrations may occur in the intended target area.

Acid deposition

Space does not permit anything more than a very brief discussion of this important topic and, for more detail, the reader is referred to the first Report of the UK Review Group on Acid Rain.[8] This Group was set up by DoE to (i) examine the distribution of acidity in the UK on the basis of data up to 1980 (ii) assess the quality of available data and to examine the evidence for trends with time and (iii) assess the need for further research programmes.

One of the important conclusions from this report was that the areas with the largest depositions were in Cumbria, the West Central Highlands and the Southern Uplands of Scotland where the annual wet deposition of H^+ was in the range 0.075-0.15 gm^{-2} year^{-1} which is of the same order as in regions of Scandinavia and North America. An important

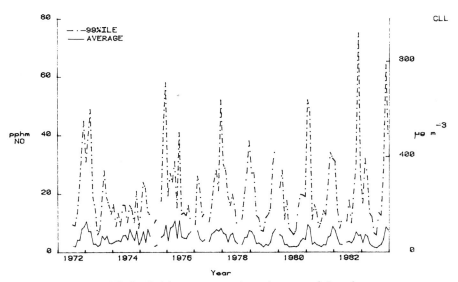

Figure 7. Nitric Oxide concentrations in central London.

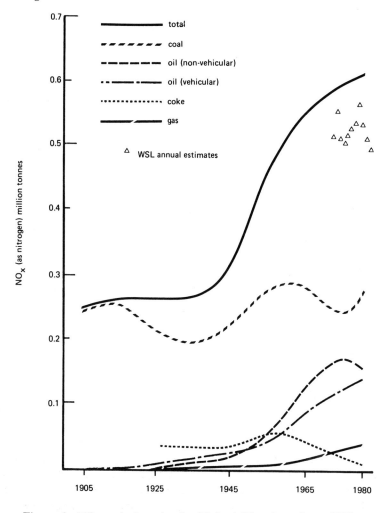

Figure 8. NO$_x$ emissions in the United Kingdom from 1905.

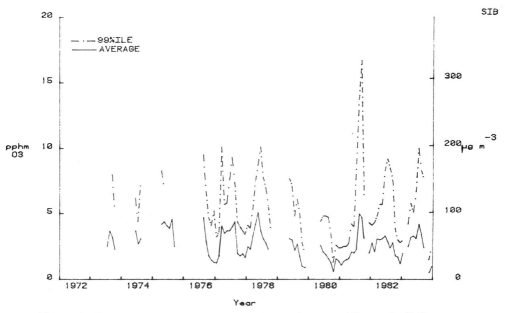

Figure 9. Ozone concentrations at WSL's rural site at Sibton, Suffolk.

recommendation of the Group was that monitoring and analysis protocols be set up to ensure comparability and quality of any future data on rainfall composition in the UK. This is an appropriate point to note that the Group has also recommended that new UK monitoring networks be set up and these are discussed below, together with future developments in monitoring for other pollutants.

Future activities

Monitoring networks for acid deposition

Following the recommendations of the Review Group on Acid Rain, DoE has asked WSL to set up two national monitoring networks for precipitation composition. The first, the Primary Network, will be a long-term baseline network of ten sites, shown in Figure 10, providing daily samples using wet-only collectors. Analyses for H^+, NH_4^+, Na^+, K^+, Ca^{2+}, Mg^{2+}, NO_3^-, Cl^-, and SO_4^{2-} will be carried out and SO_2, NO_2 and particulate sulphate will also be measured. The second network, the Secondary Network, will comprise 50-60 sites and will provide weekly samples using a common design of bulk collector with analyses being performed for H^+, NH_4^+, Na^+, PO_4^-, Na^+, NO_3^-, and SO_4^{2-}. The main purpose of the secondary network is to provide a reasonably comprehensive spatial coverage of the UK.

NO_x and ozone monitoring

Considerable attention over the past year has been devoted to background NO_x and ozone monitoring. The tenth report of the Royal Commission on Environmental Pollution, and the report of the House of Commons Select Committee on the Environment, both highlighted the paucity of monitoring of these pollutants, and the government in its responses accepted the need to expand the network. DoE asked WSL to make proposals for an enlarged network and these were discussed at an expert meeting early in 1985. The recommendation from that meeting was for a national network of about

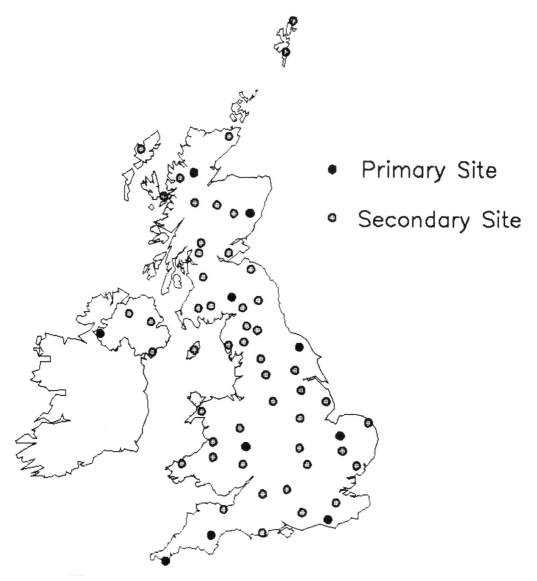

Figure 10. United Kingdom precipitation composition monitoring networks.

17 stations over the UK, and Figure 11 shows the location of stations. WSL has designed the remote stations to be fully automatic in operation, with monitoring data transmitted down British Telecom lines to the computer Local Area Network at WSL, and daily automatic calibration of gas monitors. In this way the data will be more accurate, the capture rate will be higher, and the cost will be lower, than using semi-automatic equipment which needs frequent intervention.

Two of the automatic stations will be set up by mid-1986, and thereafter they will be commissioned at the rate of about 4-5 per year, so that by mid-1988 the network will be complete. The process may be accelerated if the Central Electricity Generating Board, who are also considering expanding their monitoring, choose to instrument two or three of the network sites.

The DoE has set up a Photooxidants Review Group (similar in nature to the Review

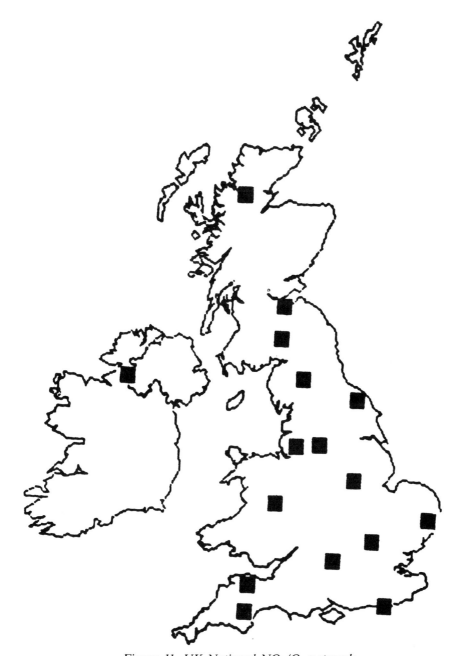

Figure 11. UK National NO_x/O_3 network.

Group on Acid Rain, composed of experts from government laboratories, industry and universities) to oversee the task and prepare a report in the same mould as the report on Acid Rain.[8] This Group may also go on to make recommendations for changes to the monitoring network where necessary, and to co-ordinate activities in the various laboratories.

Monitoring for the European Commission Directive on NO_2

In March 1985, a new EEC Directive on NO_2 concentrations was agreed. The Directive requires that the limit value of 200 μgm^{-3} of NO_2 for the 98 percentile of hourly values measured over a year shall not be exceeded. Hourly NO_2 measurements, using the chemiluminescent detectors specified by the Commission, is quite a different proposition from daily SO_2 measurements using wet chemistry. Each site will cost some Stg£20,000-£30,000 to set up. The DoE is at present in the process of selecting a number of sites where permanent monitoring stations will be established; probably about six in urban areas and possibly another three in industrial locations where NO_2 levels are expected to be relatively high.

Motor vehicles emit NO, which is converted to NO_2 quite rapidly; heavily trafficked sites will therefore be among those with the highest NO_2 levels. The cities where we intend to monitor will be chosen on the basis of population density — as good an indicator of traffic density as any, although we will be using actual traffic statistics where these are available.

Harwell, in conjunction with the Greater London Council and many LAs, has already completed a year long survey of NO_2 in Greater London using diffusion tubes, a simple but effective technique, to produce a map of NO_2 contours across London. Two areas of highest NO_2 levels have been identified; and these areas are being looked at more closely to decide on suitable permanent monitoring sites.

Similar diffusion tube surveys, but of a more limited duration, will be carried out in other cities, probably including Glasgow, Liverpool and Greater Manchester, which will allow identification of sites in these cities. To ensure that, by using population density as an indicator, we have not missed any important towns or cities, WSL will be enlisting the help of LAs to expose diffusion tubes at some urban smoke and SO_2 National Survey sites, for several months.

References

1. *Digest of Environmental Protection and Water Statistics, No. 7.* HMSO, 1984.
2. Directive No.80/779/EEC, Directive on air quality limit values and guide values for sulphur dioxide and suspended particulates. *Official Journal of the European Communities,* No. L229, 30 August, 1980.
3. *Environmental Health Criteria 8, Sulphur Oxides and Suspended Particulate Matter,* WHO, Geneva, 1979.
4. Apling A.J., Keddie A.W.C., Weatherley M-L.P.M. and Williams M.L. *The High Pollution Episode in London, December 1975.* Warren Spring Laboratory Report LR263(AP), Stevenage, 1977.
5. Bailey M.L. and Walsh J.J. *An Inventory of Smoke and Sulphur Dioxide Emissions for Dublin.* University College Dublin Report, October 1980.
6. Williams M.L., Maughan R.A., Roberts G.H. and Timmis R.J. *The Impact on Air Quality of Power Station Development in Dublin.* Warren Spring Laboratory Report LR440(AP), Stevenage, 1983.
7. Bailey M.L. *Air Quality in Ireland — The Present Position.* An Foras Forbartha, 1984.
8. *Acid Deposition in the UK — Report of the Review Group on Acid Rain.* Warren Spring Laboratory, Stevenage, 1983.

IRISH POLICY OPTIONS

FRANK CONVERY

Resource & Environmental Policy Centre, University College, Dublin.

Introduction

In order to make sensible decisions concerning Dublin's air quality, we would ideally like to know: the present state of our city's environment; the sources of pollution; the expected future air quality; the policy options, and their costs and benefits; our international obligations; the statutory, bureaucratic and other mechanisms for implementing policy, and their effectiveness.

I will concentrate my analysis on the policy options and their costs and benefits, only touching on the other aspects as essential general background.

General background

1. Only levels of smoke (particulate matter), sulphur dioxide (SO_2) and lead are measured. The levels of other pollutants, notably nitrogen oxides (NO_x), hydrocarbons and carbon monoxide (CO), are unrecorded.

2. The European Community has established limit values for smoke and SO_2 concentrations, specified in terms of annual and winter medians, and daily limit values. Dublin has been in non-compliance with the daily limit values for smoke on a number of occasions over the past decade. For this reason, policy discussion has tended to focus almost exclusively on smoke. We must be in compliance with the Directive by 1993.

3. Michael Bailey (page 20) has given the sources of smoke and sulphur in Dublin in 1983. The predominance of the domestic source for smoke, and power station and commercial industrial sources for sulphur, are notable.

4. Since 1978, when sulphur emissions from power stations reached 36,260 tonnes per annum, they have dropped sharply to 11,900, with the conversion to gas of the power stations. However, this situation could be at least partially reversed if the ESB reverts to the use of oil.

5. Several studies have attempted to demonstrate a link between the levels of smoke and sulphur in Dublin and adverse effects on human health/mortality. While identifying and adjusting for confounding effects makes it difficult to draw definitive conclusions, these studies do not allow us to reject the hypothesis that there are such adverse effects (see page 31).

6. Reservations have been expressed about the adequacy of the air quality monitoring system. These do not question the rigour or technical competence with which the measurements are taken.

The evidence adduced for these reservations is two-fold. Firstly, while smoke emissions increased sharply in the period 1975-79, measured smoke concentrations remained relatively stable over this period. Secondly, a model constructed of the Dublin airshed, undertaken for the ESB, by staff at Warren Spring Laboratory (WSL) in England "predicted", — on the basis of the meteorological conditions, fuel consumption and its location, means of combustion, etc. — smoke concentrations which were 3.3 to 3.7 times what the monitoring system observed.[1] They suggest that the discrepancy between predicted and measured results may be in part due to difficulties with measuring very fine peat smoke, which may also overlay and obscure darker particles. However, there are numerous other potential explanations for these phenomena.

In 1983, Dublin Corporation commissioned an evaluation of their monitoring system from the WSL. With regard to smoke, this study concluded that, at 6 of the 13 monitoring sites, it was "possible that the observed concentrations at the sites mentioned above may be in error and more probably under-estimated."[2] The average observed value was 48 μg m^{-3}, while the average value calculated by WSL was 81 μg m^{-3}, 69 per cent higher. Several recommendations are made regarding standardisation of clamp size at sites, procedures to be followed when site visits are interrupted due to holidays and the like, and the sampling network required for the future. The recommendations have all been put into effect, so that it is reasonable to assume that the monitoring system is providing an adequate measure of ambient concentrations.

Policy options

The following can be identified:
1. No intervention
2. Encourage the installation of smoke reducing appliances
3. Accelerate the penetration of natural gas
4. Smokeless zones
5. Other options

No intervention

This would be appropriate if either the cost of intervention exceeded any resulting benefit, if we had no international obligations to consider, or if natural market and technological forces were going in any event to eliminate the problem automatically, i.e. without intervention.

Evaluation: We are in non-compliance with the European Community limit values for smoke which specify that 98 per cent of the daily values should fall below 250 μg/m^3, and with the additional requirement that this value is not exceeded for more than 3 consecutive days. In general, we have complied with the annual and winter median limit values. However, this is little consolation, as it is the "extreme events" which cause most of the problems, not the average or medians.

In looking to the future, the financial attractiveness of the open fire with backboiler (which accounts for over three quarters of solid fuel users) is such that market incentives alone are unlikely to effect a large scale shift in use in the short to medium term. In Table 1 we can see the average operating costs of an open fire with backboiler, and the average capital and operating costs of switching to alternatives (single room). It is clear that there is little financial incentive to make such a shift. However, the reader should bear in mind that these are averages. There will certainly be instances at the margin where the relative costs favour a shift. In addition, there are non-financial considerations — aesthetic, convenience, custom, etc. — which influence choice.

For an open fire without a backboiler, the financial advantage of shifting to alternative systems is overwhelming. However, it is likely that many such fireplaces are used

Table 1: Average costs (IR£) of operating open fire with backboiler, and the capital and operating costs of shifting to alternatives, December 1984.

System	Capital	Operating
Open Fire with Backboiler	—	132
Closed Stove (House Coal or Anthracite)	400	95
Flued gas room heater	300	161
Electric Storage Heater	302	128

Source: Derived from data sheets of Energy Services, IIRS.

only for "social" reasons, i.e. they are not the main source of heat, while many of the remaining households with such fireplaces are so poor that the capital costs of investing in an alternative can prove an insurmountable barrier, regardless of the attractive paybacks.

The fall in real after-tax family income which has occurred over the past few years also favours the status quo, as it limits the availability of discretionary capital for investing in alternative point systems, and central heating. This, together with rising unemployment, also in effect reduces the opportunity cost of people's time, so that the attractiveness of converting to labour-saving systems such as natural gas is correspondingly diminished.

Over the next five years, we may see some modest recovery in real take-home pay, and this, together with the likely increase in the numbers of families with both spouses working outside the home, will result in some shift to central heating and to "convenience" fuels such as natural gas. This should at least stabilise smoke emissions at 1985/86 levels. However, I conclude that over the next three to five years, such shifting will be modest in scope, and will not of itself be sufficient to ensure compliance with the European Community's limit values. The issue then is what mix of strategies we should adopt. The strategies which I consider below are not mutually exclusive.

Install smoke-reducing appliances

This has been advocated by Coal Information Services, who argue that:
A standard coal burning appliance, with an after-burner effectively burning the volatiles, gives higher efficiencies, and smoke-reductions up to 80 per cent over existing backboiler appliances. The unit cost is only marginally more expensive than a standard backboiler unit or open fire.... Work is in progress in developing a system which can be fitted to existing fireplaces.[3]

This is a potentially very beneficial development, since it would confer both financial and environmental benefits. However, it will have to prove itself to consumers commercially and technically in day-to-day operation.

Installing such devices in new housing would certainly be effective in reducing emissions. However, the capital costs which have to be incurred to retro-fit such devices mean that they are unlikely to be fitted to existing backboilers without some form of subsidy and regulation.

Accelerate the penetration of natural gas (and electricity)

In Great Britain, the process of going "smokeless" in many cities has involved almost universal switching to natural gas, and this is attributed in part to a gas pricing policy which made natural gas very financially attractive to consumers. How viable is this alternative in the case of Dublin?

Annual coal consumption by the domestic sector falls in the range of 250,000 — 350,000 tonnes, and peat intake is of the order of 50,000 tonnes. Applying energy equivalence factors — 264 therms per tonne of coal, 150 therms per tonne of peat (assuming 50 per cent turf, 50 per cent briquettes) — to these quantities, we find a total gross energy equivalence amounting to about 100 million therms. However, adjusting for efficiency differentials in combustion would bring the gas "required" to substitute for the solid fuel down to about 85 million therms.

Two issues must be addressed in order to evaluate this strategy: what amount of solid fuel must be "taken out" in order to achieve the desired reduction in smoke emissions? What gas price decrease would be necessary in order to achieve the required substitution of gas for solid fuel?

In the absence of an air shed model, it is difficult to answer the first question. I assume arbitrarily that substituting gas for 40 per cent of current solid fuel consumption, i.e. equivalent to 34 million therms, would suffice.

The price reduction necessary to achieve this substitution is very difficult to estimate. In order to achieve large scale conversion from an open fire backboiler to a single gas room heater, the reduction in gas price would have to be very large, i.e. of the order of 50 per cent. However, in the U.K., the pattern favoured in many instances was to go from a single solid fuel burner to gas fired central heating. The relative average costs of central heating alternatives are as follows:

Table 2: Cost of central heating systems, Dublin, December 1984.

	Capital Costs of change from open fire to	Total operating costs per annum
Closed Stove		
Coal	£1300 — £2500	£663
Anthracite	£1300 — £2500	£658
Peat	£1300 — £2500	£500
Oil	£1700 — £2500	£686
Electricity	n.a.	£896
Gas	£1300 — £2500[1]	£667

Assumption: Room heated to mean temp. of 15°C. Fully insulated, summer hot water heated electrically, cost of elective cooking included.
[1]But special promotional conversion rates are available
Source: Energy Services, IIRS.

In view of the data in Table 2, it is surprising to find that, in 1983, virtually no gas-fired central heating was installed in new housing (Table 3). However, this may change as the promotional efforts of Dublin Gas intensify and as the grid is extended.

For purposes of illustration, I assume that a targetted 40 per cent reduction in the 1985 gas price to consumers — taken as 88p per therm (the "economy" rate) — which would amount to 35.2p per therm, would be sufficient to substitute for 40 per cent of existing solid fuel consumption. We can see from Table 1 that such a gas price reduction would reduce operative costs for a flued gas room heater to £96.6 per annum. The annual operating savings achieved over an open fire with backboiler (£35.4) would certainly encourage a significant level of gas heater installation. If, in the absence of this "cheap gas" strategy, the State would in effect store the gas and sell it at 1985 prices, then the cost

Table 3: Central heating in private estate houses, Dublin, 1983

	% of Total
Oil	3
Oil and Solid Fuel	23
Solid Fuel	73
Gas	1
Electricity	0
None	0
	100

Note: Central heating is not installed in local authority housing. Two fireplaces — one with backboiler — are installed. Every house is on gas mains, so that tenants have a choice of gas or electricity for cooking. They can also usually bring in gas heat at their own expense.

today is the discounted value of future revenues foregone. If, for example, such a storage period would be 15 years, and all of the "stored" gas would be used in that year, then the total costs today of having cheap gas over the intervening 15 year period are:

$$34 \times 0.352 \times 15 \times 1/(1.05)^{15} = £86 \text{ million}$$

if the real interest is five per cent. This represents the present value of foregone earnings by the citizenry who own the Kinsale Head Field.

Evaluation: It is clear from the analysis above that the pyramid of assumptions which I made concerning consumer response to price and quantity shifts requires validation; this would be very difficult to achieve.

In addition, once a price change for one fuel is "forced" into a system, it will trigger a chain reaction in competing fuels. With regard to air quality in Dublin, electricity and LPG are also "clean", and an analogous analysis could have been conducted. Should they also be "encouraged"? Some investment in infrastructure would be necessary in order to bring gas to some outer areas, and this has not been costed. My analysis assumes that the discount price is confined to the target householders representing 40 per cent solid fuel use. While this should be technically feasible, in practice it may well prove difficult to avoid spreading the benefit more widely, with consequent ramifications for future earnings foregone and quantity consumed.

If a further commercial gas field were to be discovered, which extended the life of Irish gas for 30 years, then the opportunity cost of the gas option — using the assumptions made above — would fall to £42 million. Gas also has the great advantage that it is virtually free of sulphur.

Smokeless zones

This is the approach adopted in the U.K., whereby a particular neighbourhood is designated "smokeless", and it is an offence for smoke to be emitted from any chimney or building. Conversion grants covering 70 per cent of approved costs are available and, for individuals on supplementary assistance or who can otherwise demonstrate need, the grant can cover the total cost.

This process of designating smokeless zones has been underway in Belfast since 1969, and about 55,000 dwellings (2/3 of the housing stock) are now in smoke control areas. The total cost of converting the most recent approved area of 3800 houses was Stg£1,018,000, or Stg£268 (IR£335) per house. However, this includes houses which are already "smokeless". The average cost of converting a house is estimated at £470 (Sterling) or £587 (Irish). Applying the average cost per house of £587 to 40 per cent of the 200,000 houses in Dublin using solid fuel to a significant extent (i.e. to 80,000 houses), we find a *total cost* (private and public), of £46.96 million. This does not include costs of administration.*

*Administration:***

The Belfast programme is administered by four inspectors and two technical assistants. Total costs of administration including salaries, travel, accounting etc. in 1985/86 are estimated at Stg£115,000 (IR£144,000).

The area to be designated is first surveyed by technicians, and each building is inventoried as to existing heating system (number of fires in regular use, and the feasible "smokeless" alternatives), including the preference of householders. Each designated zone has in order of 2000 — 4000 houses; 4000 houses comprise a year's work for the unit.

Once the city council has approved a designation, it goes for approval to the Department of Environment. Once this is forthcoming, householders are informed by letter concerning the designation of the area as a smoke control zone, what their fuel and combustion choices etc. are, what the grant allowable will be. Such letters should ideally be sent out in May — June, and the work can then be completed by the following May — June.

About 90 per cent of householders convert to solid fuel systems, of which 70 per cent are room heaters (stoves) and the balance fan assisted or "Baki" (underfloor draught) systems. The remainder are mainly electricity conversions.

There is very little resistance to designation; typically fewer than ten householders in a 2000 — 4000 zone object, perhaps because the operating costs of smokeless and conventional are the same, and a 100 per cent capital grant is available for those in need.

Enforcement can be a problem for those householders who install underfloor draught fires, since they can burn bituminous fuel. However, warnings have proved sufficient in most instances: no case has ever been taken to court.

Forty per cent of the total conversion cost is borne by Central Government, while 30 per cent is paid by the local authority. If 100 per cent funding is provided, the balance outstanding (30 per cent) must be provided by the local authority.

Evaluation: This system has the potential advantage of being able to immediately address the localities of greatest need. It is flexible in that it allows householders to make up their own minds concerning choice between solid fuel, gas, electricity, etc.

It is administratively relatively expensive, requiring intensive house surveys, visits, etc. It takes effect slowly. If 4000 houses were converted annually in Dublin, it would take 20 years to "do" 80,000 houses. On this basis, the annual *total* conversion cost would be £2.35 million, of which probably close to £2 million would have to come from the Exchequer. In addition, there would be annual administrative costs of up to £200,000. The total present value of these costs come to £32 million.

---

*(Costs were provided by Jim Lamont and David Dixon, Department of Environment, N. Ireland. Personal communication, November 27, 1985.)

**(All information in this section has been provided by Cecil Alison, Smoke Control Section, Belfast City Council. Personal communication, November 28, 1985.)

Other options

I have concentrated on smoke and domestic heating, because this seems to be the priority at the moment. However, it is important not to lose sight of the fact that sulphur can still be an issue. Diesel burning in vehicles contributes 15 per cent of smoke; to those who practise the noble art of cycling, this can be a source of extreme discomfort. Lead emissions are likely to diminish slowly over time, as low lead and then lead-free petrol are introduced. However, there can still be threat, especially to young children in inner city areas, when lead has accumulated in dust and paint particles.

If households were to use smokeless fuel on those (relatively few) days when the weather was "bad" from a pollution point of view, this would certainly be the most cost-effective approach to cleaning up the air. The availability now of smokeless fuels which burn very well in an open fire enhances the possibility of this option. The main problems are that the days of pollution-inducing weather have to be predicted, and households must then as a group use "smokeless" on those days.

Summary

The data

There has been a lack of confidence by some independent scientists in the credibility of the Dublin monitoring system. Their concerns will be allayed by the implementation of the recommendations from WSL.

The options

The *Do Nothing* option is not really feasible, for at least two related reasons. We have binding commitments under European Community law, with which we are not at present in compliance. Secondly, the pattern of heating systems being installed in new housing (73 per cent solid fuel central heating in private, all open fire with back boiler in local authority housing) indicates that the situation will not improve in the short-to-medium term (five years). As real incomes grow in the future, we can, however, expect substantial penetration by natural gas.

Smoke-reducing appliances are being developed which early tests show could reduce smoke emissions by 50 per cent or more. If installed in new houses, these would clearly make a beneficial impact on the problem.

Providing *cheap gas* to open fire users would have a beneficial effect, because gas is a very clean fuel. However, we don't know what price reduction it would take to achieve, say, a 40 per cent reduction in solid fuel consumption on open fires. I assume that a 40 per cent reduction in price would suffice. The cost of this strategy is the discounted value of the revenue foregone: this is estimated at £86 million. If a further gas field were discovered, so that the field-life extended to 30 years, the cost falls to £42 million. The costs of extending the gas grid are not included.

The main problem with this approach is that other fuel systems which are "clean" in Dublin, such as electricity and LPG, would be discriminated against and there would be a clamour for "parity". It might also prove difficult to confine the "cheap" gas to zones of poor air quality.

The declaration of *smokeless zones,* and the implementation of grant aided conversion is the approach to smoke pollution followed in the UK. In Belfast, total conversion costs per house average £587 and administrative costs about £48 per house. If 4000 were converted per annum, total costs (including administration) would amount to £2.55 million (1985£) and take about 20 years to cover 40 per cent of the solid fuel burning housing stock.

Recommendations

A mix of strategies, some somewhat experimental in nature, is what is required. Concentrate on the areas where the problem is most severe. Refine the data on these areas. Use an "early warning" system to predict pollution-prone weather, and use the media to advocate the use of smokeless fuels on those days. Test the smoke-reducing device in a new housing development; introduce a prototype smokeless zone of 4000 houses in one of the worst affected areas. *If* a new gas field is developed, bring down the price of gas at least in the priority areas. Install smokeless fuel burning systems in all new local authority housing and require the same for new private housing, at least in those zones where non-compliance is judged to be a severe and continuing problem.

Acknowledgement

The research on which this paper is based was funded by the National Board for Science and Technology, now EOLAS. This support is gratefully acknowledged. The contents are the responsibility of the author alone.

References

1. Williams, M.L. *et al. The Input on Air Quality of Power Station Development in Dublin.* Warren Spring Laboratory, Dept of Industry, Stevenage, 1983.
2. Spanton, A.M. and McInnes, G. *Monitoring Network Assessment for the Dublin Area.* Warren Spring Laboratory, Dept of Industry, Stevenage, 4, 1986.
3. Coal Information Services. *Towards a Planned Improvement in Dublin's Air Quality.* Dublin, 19, 1985.
4. O'Connor, Eamon. Coal Information Services, Personal Communication, December 1987.

SEMINAR CONCLUSIONS*

The seminar recognises that the nature and extent of air pollution in Dublin is sufficiently serious to present a problem in the areas of health, amenity, and the deterioration of historic and other buildings. This requires positive corrective action now, including a public information programme.

Much of the problem arises from burning solid fuels in open fires. Alleviation is possible by fuel substitution and the choice of proper appliances.

Progress can be achieved immediately by the introduction and implementation of appropriate air quality legislation covering, inter alia, domestic sources. The conference heard that substantial improvements could be achieved at reasonable cost.

*Drafted by the organisers and approved by a large majority of the participants.

INDEX

Acknowledgements

The production of this booklet was a team effort. I am indebted to my colleagues Brian Hall, Max Jones, Andy Vince, and Peter Warden for the manner in which they addressed this not too easy task, and to Dorothy Chipchase for her administration and record keeping during all of the discussions which preceded writing.

A work of this nature draws on a wide range of materials from a multitude of sources, the origins of which are buried in the sands of time. We have drawn actively from the work of the BAF Startrack/Pacesetter development group, and from the special regional work of Athletics Coaching Northern Division to supplement our own experience.

We have also drawn, to a lesser extent, upon the work of Len Almond, Director of Physical Education, Loughborough University of Technology, and his team working on behalf of the Health Education Authority, David Edgecombe, Senior Lecturer emeritus at the School of Education, Exeter University, and Graham Tanner, past Head of Physical Education, Wootton Basset School, Swindon, Wilts. We are most grateful for their co-operation.

Last, but not least, we are grateful for the help of John Deacon who brought a host of drawings, of varying origins and quality, into the unified whole which we see here.

Carl Johnson (Editor)
B.A.F. National Coach and
Chief Education Officer

Cover photographs
The B.A.F. is grateful for the kind cooperation of:
      Eileen Langsley of Supersport
      A.P.A. on behalf of Trustee Savings Bank
      Scottish Sports Council
and also for the use of photographs which show Sports Hall Athletics and the StarTrack Scheme in action.

ATHLETICS COACH

The quarterly coaching journal of the B.A.F.

Details from:

**The British Athletics Coaching Office,
225a Bristol Road, Edgbaston,
Birmingham B5 7UB**

Tel: 0121 440 5000   Fax: 0121 440 0555

Contents

Preface

Athletics is really several different sports rolled into one. Shot Putting is very different from Pole Vaulting, and attracts quite different types of people. Similarly Sprinting and Marathon, whilst both involving running, are quite dissimilar in the manner in which it is done, and the types of individuals that they attract. Hurdling and Long Jumping, whilst requiring good sprinting ability, make quite different technical demands of the performer and coach.

The knowledge needed to teach and coach, at a certain point, becomes quite specific to each event. It was thus right and logical that as qualifications in athletics coaching evolved, they did so as a series of compartmentalised, event focused abilities.

The need for a booklet like this has been apparent for some time. It arises from the fact that children's involvement in sport, and motivation to learn, operate in ways quite different from that of adults; yet young athletes form large, sometimes majority, groups in clubs. However, the most effective learning mode for these groups comes close to that which brings success in school.

This booklet also recognises the fact that many coaches working in clubs do so predominantly, or even entirely, with young athletes. They are enthusiastic about what they do, and are perfectly happy to channel all their energies into this work. They are not particularly interested in becoming specialist coaches to adult, or even developing athletes, and being limited to one event, or a small group of related events.

Since specialisation at too early an age goes against the long term best interests of young athletes, coaches and teachers working with them need to be equipped with knowledge across all events, but not to an advanced level. This is what the Coaching Young Athletes booklet sets out to do. It addresses the needs of those working in the Foundation and Participation developmental bands now recognised across all sport in the United Kingdom, i.e. from roughly ages 7/8 to 12/13.

Whilst British Athletic Federation booklets are written mainly to inform coaches they have always had a secondary purpose – that of conveying technical knowledge to performers, particularly those unfortunate enough not to have access to a personal coach. Modern BAF booklets also address the particular needs of our coaching award scheme. This one provides the source material concerning activities and practices for coaches preparing for the BAF Club Coach – Level 2 – Coaching Young Athletes award. It does not contain the supporting coaching theory necessary for that award. For this a further publication, the Coaching Young Athletes Award – Coaching Theory Manual, obtainable from BAF Publications, is necessary.

Having *fun* with athletics

INTRODUCTION

ATHLETICS' GAMES provide a way of ensuring that young athletes *enjoy* their first few years in the sport. It need not stop there! Older athletes can get a great deal of enjoyment and a considerable amount of work out of training in this way. Games can be introduced into the conditioning phase of the training programme to great effect, increasing enthusiasm and through it the amount of work accomplished.

COMPETITIONS FOR FUN

Competitions can be organised so that they address:
- how FAR
- how HIGH, or
- how FAST, plus for our purposes;
- how MANY
- how OFTEN, and also
- how GOOD.

  The latter provides a measure of technical excellence.

The athlete can also compete against:
- personal records
- standards
- peers
- extrinsic records
- other teams, and
- his/her-self.

  It is motivationally useful for the coach to keep a record of all results achieved in these games and publish them, on the club notice board.

Typical of these types of competitions are:
- straight competitions
- handicap competitions
- aggregate score competitions
- team total competitions
- individual records
- percentage improvement.

A coaching group or class result sheet could therefore include:
- the Top Ten individuals, or teams
- the Most Improved individuals, or teams, and
- a league table.

If the same games are used, under similar conditions for a variety of groups or classes, it is possible to participate in inter-group or inter-class competition without them actually meeting. This can even include postal competition between groups many miles apart.

GAME DESIGN

The following considerations are important:

1. EFFICIENCY
   MAMT – Maximum Activity in the Minimum Time, or . . . don't keep the children waiting around for their turn.

2. EFFECT
   Does the game achieve the effect that you require?

3. FATIGUE
   Can the children complete the session without distress? Remember . . . skill deteriorates as fatigue increases.

4. SKILL
   If the skill element is to be high, fatigue must be low.

5. RULES
   Effective games need simple rules.

6. SAFETY
   All competitions must be safe for competitors, spectators and the coach.
   The K.I.S.S. principle - Keep It Safe and Simple is most appropriate.

TYPES OF GAMES

They can be categorised as follows:

(a) WARM UP and WARM DOWN ACTIVITIES, including . . .
   - General Stretching exercises
   - Partner Stretching (which needs careful supervision)
   - Paired Competitions
   - Team Games
   - Non-specific Relays.

(b) EVENT SPECIFIC ACTIVITIES, including . . .
   - Speed Games
   - Endurance Games and Relays
   - Pace Judgement Games
   - Throwing and Jumping Games
   - Governing Body Award Scheme activities.

(c) POTTED SPORTS

WARM UP and WARM DOWN ACTIVITIES
GENERAL STRETCHING and PARTNER STRETCHING ACTIVITIES
N.B. ALL STRETCHING SHOULD BE DONE SLOWLY AND CAREFULLY

Fig. W1
NECK STRETCH

Head side to side.

Do not circle.

Fig. W5
SHOULDER STRETCH

Arms circling
forwards,
backwards,
and in opposite
directions.

Fig. W2
SIDE STRETCH

Trunk side to side,
and circling.

Fig. W6
THIGH STRETCH

Form a bow.

Keep head
shoulders
up.

W A L L

Fig. W3
ARM/SHOULDER
STRETCH

Arms
upwards
stretch.

Fig. W7
ACHILLES
STRETCH
Keep one foot off the
floor with one leg
straight: press the
heel down
and back
until it is flat on
the ground.

W A L L

Fig. W4
UPPER CHEST
STRETCH

Arms
sideways
and
backwards
stretch.

Fig. W8
BACK STRETCH

Back
curl over.

Fig. W9
HAMSTRING STRETCH

Reach slowly
down and touch toes
without bending legs.
Can also be done with
legs crossed.

Fig. W13
HIP/QUAD/ACHILLES STRETCH

Front knee over front foot. Keep a wide
thigh split with rear knee on the ground.
Push rear knee up and back, keeping hips
level.

Fig. W10
HAMSTRING STRETCH

Sit with legs wide apart. Reach forwards
with both hands and grasp one ankle.
Hold the position for 6 - 10 secs.
Repeat on the other side, then with both
ankles.

Fig. W14
BACK and HIP STRETCH

Lie on tummy grasping ankles.
Lift chest and thighs
off the ground
and hold.

Fig. W11
THIGH/HAM STRETCH

Legs wide astride.
Push heel
back to the
ground, and
hips down.

Fig. W15
BACK LIFT

Lie on back and lift hips as high as possible.
Circle hips to right and to left.

Fig. W12
THIGH/BACK STRETCH

Maintain
hip split.
Gently arch
the body.
Hold for
6 - 10 secs.

Fig. W16
BACK CURL

From back
lying curl up
and clasp
knees.

Fig. W17
HAMSTRING CURL

From back lying, raise and support the hips. Stretch both legs overhead, towards the ground, then straighten them.

Fig. W18
BACK & SHOULDER STRETCH

(a) Kneel, with arms forwards and straight, with hands on the ground, and nose almost touching it. Move the body forwards keeping nose close to the ground.
(b) Arch the body up keeping hips on the ground.
Then curl back to the starting position.

Fig. W19
BACK HYPER-EXTENSION

Lie on tummy.
Lift head, shoulders and feet as high as possible, and HOLD.

Fig. W20
BACK/SHOULDER/HAMSTRING STRETCH

From hands and knees, raise an arm and opposite leg straight, and HOLD.
Then try it with arm and leg on SAME side.

Fig. W21
SHOULDERS and BACK STRETCH

Lean against the wall with knees slightly bent, and hands slightly overhead, with fingers pointing down.
Push with arms so that the body arches, and HOLD.

Fig. W22
HAMSTRING STRETCH

Crouch with hands on the ground.
Slowly straighten the legs and HOLD.
Keep hands on the ground.

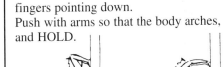

Fig. W23
SHOULDER STRETCH

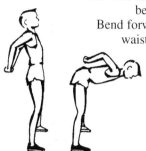

Feet wide astride and arms behind the back. Bend forwards from the waist keeping back straight. Move both arms away from the body and HOLD.

Fig. W24
SHOULDER STRETCH

Interlock the fingers of both hands. Turn them outwards. Raise both arms above the head. Press backwards and HOLD.

Fig. W25
LOWER BACK &
SHOULDER STRETCH

Raise a straight leg whilst lying on back. Keep shoulders flat against the ground. Press the raised leg across the body to touch the ground on the opposite side.

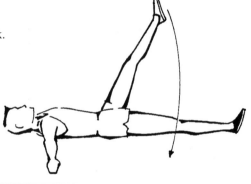

Fig. W26. SHOULDER STRETCH - take care - must be taken seriously

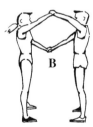

| Face partner and hold hands | Lower arms on one side | Walk through the arch | Pass back to back |

Lift other arms and walk back to the starting position

PARTNER EXERCISES AND PAIRED GAMES

Fig. W27
BACK-to-BACK SQUATS

Stand back to back.
Link arms. Squat and stand up.
Repeat several times SLOWLY.

Fig. W30
BACK LIFTS

One partner lies face down while the other holds their heels. Lying partner lifts head and shoulders off the ground.

Fig. W28
PUSHING ACTIVITIES

Face partner and place hands on their shoulders.
Try to push partner backward.

Fig. W31
PULLING CIRCLE

Stand toe
to toe.
Hold hands.
Lean back.
Circle slowly.
DON'T BE
SILLY.

Fig. W29.
PULLING ACTIVITIES

Set up as in W26, but holding hands or wrists. Pull partner forwards, or, stand sideways on to partner, and grasp their right hand with your left. Brace your left foot sideways against your partner's right foot. Bend legs and pull!

Fig. W32
PUSHING CIRCLE

Place hands
on partner's
shoulders.
Lean forwards.
Circle slowly.
DON'T BE SILLY.

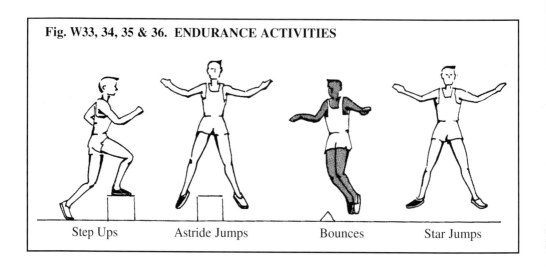

Fig. W33, 34, 35 & 36. ENDURANCE ACTIVITIES

| Step Ups | Astride Jumps | Bounces | Star Jumps |

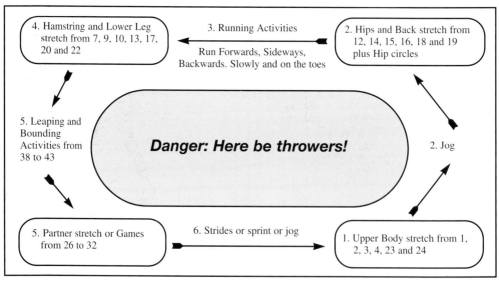

4. Hamstring and Lower Leg stretch from 7, 9, 10, 13, 17, 20 and 22

3. Running Activities

Run Forwards, Sideways, Backwards. Slowly and on the toes

2. Hips and Back stretch from 12, 14, 15, 16, 18 and 19 plus Hip circles

5. Leaping and Bounding Activities from 38 to 43

Danger: Here be throwers!

2. Jog

5. Partner stretch or Games from 26 to 32

6. Strides or sprint or jog

1. Upper Body stretch from 1, 2, 3, 4, 23 and 24

The numbers indicated at each stage relate to exercises previously listed, which in themselves are a small selection from the hundreds available. Further reference should be made to the BAF booklet 'Mobility Training'.

N.B. When selecting exercises for youngsters ensure that the exercise does not place too great a strain on young joints and muscles.

Game 3 – Capture the Flag

Game objective	An invasion game in which teams attempt to enter another's territory and 'steal' a flag or cone whilst defending their own.
Rules	Teams begin in their own territory wearing a braid 'tail' tucked in their shorts. Participants can move anywhere, so long as their 'tail' remains intact. Opponents 'tails' can be removed, consigning them to 'prison'. Prisoners can be released either: ● by skipping 100 times in prison, or ● by being touched by a free member of their own team. Captured 'tails' are stored at the centre spot to be collected by freed prisoners.

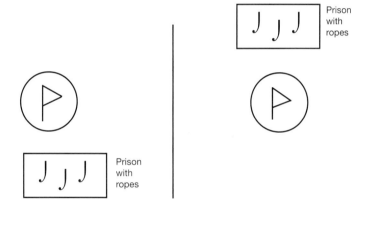

Equipment	2 marker flags or cones, skipping ropes, a hoop and sufficient team bands/braids of different colours for all players.
Organisation	Split the group into 2 teams, and issue each with braid 'tails' of a different colour. Divide the playing area into equal halves, and place the flag/cone at the far end of each. Mark out the prison compounds in a corner of both territories, placing some skipping ropes in each. Place the hoop at the centre as the 'tail' store.
Progression	a. Ban too close defending of the flag/cone.

Game 4 – Orienteering Codebreaker

Game objective	A simplified orienteering activity to promote running and walking in which players are challenged to decode a secret message.
Rules	Players can work alone, or in pairs sharing a worksheet. They break the code by matching numbers to corresponding letters, which they enter on their worksheet. Time should be permitted at the start so that tactical decisions can be made.

P	L	A	Y		F	R	I	S	B	E	E
1	4	6	9		18	8	5	13	14	12	12
W	I	T	H		Y	O	U	R			
2	5	7	10		16	17	15	8			
P	A	R	T	N	E	R					
3	6	8	7	12	12	8					

Organisation	Distribute cones/flags, bearing both a number and a letter, randomly around the working area but within sight of the start. Leave some blank.
Equipment	30 activity cones, or posts, labels, marker pens, Codebreaker worksheets and individual pens/pencils.
Progression	It is possible to make the Codebreaker message lead into the next activity.

ORIENTEERING CARD DETAILS

CHECK POINT CARDS 12 OFF – ACTUAL SIZE A4, PLASTIC COVERED

1		2		3		4		5		6	
A	- 12	A	- 10	A	- 7	A	- 11	A	- F	A	- 1
B	- 4	B	- 7	B	- 1	B	- F	B	- 11	B	- 10
C	- 4	C	- 5	C	- 12	C	- 9	C	- 8	C	- 3
D	- 6	D	- 12	D	- 8	D	- 11	D	- 2	D	- 10
E	- 9	E	- 8	E	- 12	E	- 7	E	- F	E	- 11
F	- 10	F	- 11	F	- 9	F	- 8	F	- 7	F	- 1
G	- 5	G	- 9	G	- 10	G	- F	G	- 12	G	- 7
H	- 11	H	- 10	H	- F	H	- 12	H	- 9	H	- 4

7		8		9		10		11		12	
A	- 9	A	- 5	A	- 6	A	- 8	A	- 3	A	- 2
B	- 9	B	- 5	B	- 6	B	- 12	B	- 2	B	- 3
C	- 11	C	- F	C	- 7	C	- 6	C	- 2	C	- 1
D	- 5	D	- 1	D	- 4	D	- F	D	- 3	D	- 9
E	- 10	E	- 5	E	- 3	E	- 2	E	- 4	E	- 6
F	- 2	F	- 12	F	- 5	F	- 4	F	- 6	F	- F
G	- 3	G	- 6	G	- 1	G	- 4	G	- 2	G	- 8
H	- 1	H	- 3	H	- 2	H	- 7	H	- 6	H	- 8

Fig G1

COMPETITORS CARD

NAME		LETTER	
TEAM			

S E Q U E N C E	1 START		S E Q U E N C E	7	
	2			8	
	3			9	
	4			10	
	5			11	
	6			12 FINISH	

TIME		ALL CORRECT	

Fig G2

COMPETITORS CARD

Competitor carries this card and pencil and marks the sequence.
Check Point (approx size 15cm x 10cm)

Fig G3

ORGANISERS MASTER CHECK CARD

	START	SEQUENCE CHECK CARD (ROTA)											FINISH
A	4	11	3	7	9	6	1	12	2	10	8	5	F
B	8	5	11	2	7	9	6	10	12	3	1	4	F
C	10	6	3	12	1	4	9	7	11	2	5	8	F
D	7	5	2	12	9	11	4	3	8	1	6	10	F
E	1	9	3	12	6	11	4	7	10	2	8	5	F
F	3	9	5	7	2	11	6	1	10	4	8	12	F
G	11	2	9	1	5	12	8	6	7	3	10	4	F
H	5	9	2	10	7	1	11	6	4	12	8	3	F

Game 5 – Orienteering Sprint Relay

Game objective	Good for accommodating large numbers.
Rules	All first runners start together, going to their team's first check point. *Coach starts a stopwatch.* There the next reference is given, against the team identification letter. It is copied onto the Competitor's Card (fig G2) and brought back to base, where it is checked by a Controller. If wrong he/she must return and correct. The next team member takes over the card and pencil and sets off to the second check point. The team time is recorded on returning to base after all check points have been correctly visited.

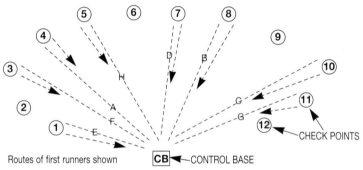

Routes of first runners shown | CB ◄—CONTROL BASE

ORIENTEERING – SPRINT RELAY FIELD LAYOUT

Organisation	Distribute cones/flags, bearing prepared Orienteering Cards (fig G1), randomly around the working area but within sight of the start. Allocate an identification letter to each team. Tell 1st runners the number reference of their first check point, which they enter in square 1 of their Competitor's Card.
Equipment	30 activity cones, or posts, labels, marker pens, Orienteering Cards, Master Check Card for the Controller (fig G3), Competitor's Cards and individual pens/pencils
Progression	a. It is possible to work in 8 teams of up to 6 runners per team b. Larger numbers can be accommodated by going through the sequence more than once. c. Don't leave people out. It doesn't matter if some teams have more members than others. d. Working without Competitor's Cards is possible if the check point number is committed to memory and verbally given to the Controller and next runner.

SECTION 2 - RUNNING & DODGING GAMES

Game 6 – 'Free and Caught' – a free running game of tag.

Game objective	Catchers attempt to 'tag' all free runners by touching them. The number of catchers will depend upon the total number in the group.
Rules	Free runners must stand still, with hands on head, when touched, until released by being touched by a free runner.
Equipment	Coloured braids sufficient for each catcher.
Organisation	Define the limits of the area to be used. It may be a gym, part or all of a Sports Hall, or a designated part of a playground, field or athletics track. Catchers wear coloured braids, or some other form of identification.
Progression	(1) Tagged runners stand with legs apart and are freed by free runners crawling through their legs. (2) Tagged runners make a bridge shape on their hands and feet and are released by free runners crawling under the bridge. (3) Tagged runners stand still with hands on head and legs apart. Before they can be released the tagged must link up with another tagged runner. They are permitted to move in order to do this. They are released by free runners crawling through the legs of BOTH.

Game 7 – Catching Tails

Game objective	To collect as many 'tails' as possible without losing your own.
Rules	Players cannot protect their own tail by holding it. They can protect it only by running and dodging. If their own tail is lost they can still continue collecting other tails.
Equipment	Coloured braids sufficient for all taking part.
Organisation	Define the limits of the area to be used. It may be a a gym, part or all of a Sports Hall, or a designated part of a playground, field or athletics track. Issue braids to each participant. Catchers wear braids around their chest whilst remainder tuck them into the waistband of their shorts or tracksuit trousers at the back, with at least half hanging out.
Progression	5 catchers snatch tails from free runners. Those who lose tails become catchers, placing the braid across their chest and the catcher becomes a free runner with tail in waistband.

Game 8 – Circle Dodge

Game objective	For the catcher to touch the person in the circle wearing the braid. The 3 in the circle try to prevent this by moving sideways (clockwise or anticlockwise).
Rules	<ul><li>If the catcher touches the player wearing the braid they exchange places.</li><li>The braid is passed on to the next person in the group in a clockwise direction.</li></ul>
Equipment	A braid for each group
Organisation	A circle drawn on ground for each group.

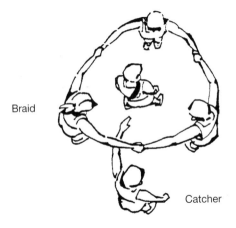

Braid

Catcher

Progression	Into Line Dodge – see Game 4.

Game 9 – Line Dodge

Game objective	For the catcher to touch the player at the end of the line.
Rules	• When the back player has been touched he/she becomes the catcher. • The catcher goes to the front of the line. • Front dodger can protect by holding arms to side. • Other dodgers must hold onto one in front with both hands. • They move as a unit.
Equipment	None
Organisation	

Catcher

Progression	(1)	1 versus 2
	(2)	1 versus 4

Game 10 – Fox and Chickens

Game objective	To get to your line before being touched by your opponent.
Rules	• Players sit on the ground, back to back with opponent, each with hands on head. • One is designated the 'FOX' whilst the other becomes the 'CHICKEN'. • When own name is called by the coach, that player chases their opponent to the opponent's 'safety' line.
Equipment	None, other than central assembly line and two distant 'safety' lines
Organisation	

```
        C                    C   F
        H                    C   F
        I                    C   F              F
        C                    C   F              O
        K                    C   F              X
        E                    C   F
        N                    C   F              L
                             C   F              I
        L                    C   F              N
        I                    C   F              E
        N                    C   F
        E                    C   F
```

Progression	None

Game 11 – Pair Tag

Game objective	To stay free for the whole game.
Rules	• Two catchers hold hands and attempt to tag the free players. • The pair must not release their hold on each other's hand. • When caught, players join hands with the free hand of one of the pair to make a catching group of three. • When a fourth player is caught the group splits to form two catching pairs. • The game ends when all have been caught, when the last pair caught can become the first catchers for the next game.
Equipment	None.
Organisation	Designate the boundaries of the playing area.
Progression	To Chain Tag in which those caught add to the size of the original group instead of splitting into pairs when a group of 4 has been formed. The chain must not break. Free players can only be caught by those at the ends of the chain.

Game 12 – Everybody Up

Game objective	To test the strength and balance of the group as they attempt to stand up together.	
Rules and Organisation	(a) IN PAIRS	• Partners face each other and join hands. • They lean back, with long arms, and sit down. • They then attempt to stand up together without releasing their grasp.
	(b) IN A GROUP	• Form a circle with hands joined. • They ALL sit down, then stand up TOGETHER, without releasing their grasp.
	(c) IN A GROUP	• Everyone sits down in two lines facing each other. • A tangle of hands is made whilst seated. • Opposite pairs are not permitted to grasp each other's hands. • When ALL hands are joined the whole group stands up together.
Progression	Invent you own variants.	

SECTION 3 - TEAM GAMES USING A BALL

Game 13 – Piggy in the Middle

Game objective	To make a set number of passes without 'piggy' in the middle touching the ball.
Rules	• If 'piggy' touches the ball the player making that pass changes places with 'piggy'. • If the target number of passes is made the player making the last pass changes places with 'piggy'.
Equipment	Four skittles and a large ball (football or netball) to each working group of players.
Organisation	Use the skittles to mark out the playing area. Choose working groups and issue one ball to each.

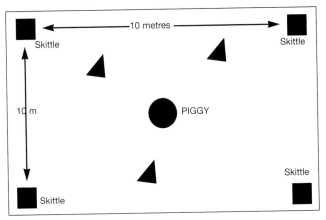

Progression	(1) 4 versus 2 (2) 5 versus 2 (3) use a small medicine ball (e.g. 2kg) instead of a large ball.

Game 14 – Ball Tag

Game objective	To stay free for as long as possible.
Rules	• One player is free. • The remainder of the group are the catchers. • One ball is passed among the catchers who must attempt to touch the free player with the ball whilst holding it. • Catchers may not run with the ball.
Equipment	Large ball such as football or netball.
Organisation	Define the boundaries of the playing area.
Progression	(1) Increase the number of balls available. (2) Time the free player, and see who stays free longest. (3) Use a small medicine ball instead of a large ball.

Game 15 – Hoop Ball

Game objective	To score a goal by getting a ball to a player of one's own side standing in the hoop.
Rules	• The game starts with a pass from the centre. • The player making a scoring pass changes places with the player in the hoop. • After a score the other side restarts the game with a pass from alongside the the hoop. • No pushing. • No running with the ball.
Equipment	Large ball (football or netball) Two hoops. Braids for one team's identification.
Organisation	No side or end line restrictions.

3 x 3

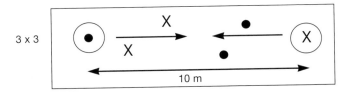

10 m

4 x 4

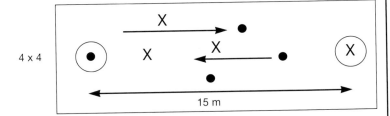

15 m

Progression	(1) 5 versus 5 (2) Replace large ball with a small medicine ball. (3) Bounce Ball - game 11.

Game 16 – Bounce Ball

Game objective	To score a goal by bouncing the ball in one of your opponents hoops.
Rules	As for Hoop Ball.
Equipment	4 hoops, one ball and braids (optional) per game.
Organisation	No side or end restrictions.

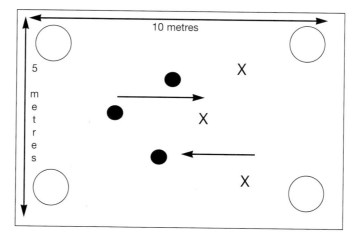

Progression	(1) 4 versus 4, or even more.
	(2) Reduce from 4 to 2 hoops.
	(3) Use 2 or more balls.
	(4) Replace large balls with small medicine balls.

Game 17 – Beat the Ball

Game objective	How many passes can be made whilst the opposing team complete a set number of laps, or How far can be run whilst the opposing team make a set number of passes.
Rules	● The runners lap outside the markers. ● Dropped passes do not count. ● Passers may be either standing or seated.
Equipment	3 skittles, 1 large ball, and 1 quoit or relay baton per game.
Organisation	Mark out a triangular course using the skittles for each game. Arrange the passing team around the three points of the triangle, and the running team at one apex. Issue quoit or baton to the running team, and ball to the passing team.

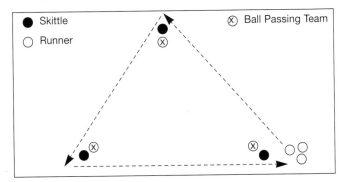

Progression	(1) Increase the number of team members: (2) Reverse the direction of passing and running. (3) Work a zigzag.

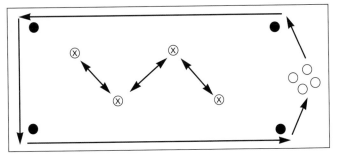

Games 18 & 19 – Bench Ball and Mat Ball

Game objective	To score a goal by passing the ball to a receiver standing on a bench, or a mat.
Rules	<ul><li>The game starts and restarts with a pass from the centre.</li><li>The receiver can move anywhere on the bench or mat.</li><li>A pass to the receiver only scores when he/she is in contact with the bench or mat.</li><li>Other team members may not move over or onto the bench or mat.</li><li>No running with the ball.</li><li>No contact.</li><li>Play can go on behind the bench or mat if they are placed away from the end line/wall.</li></ul>
Equipment	2 gym benches or landing mats, one large ball, braids (optional).
Organisation	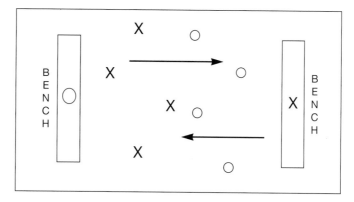
Progression	(1) Increase the numbers in the teams. (2) Introduce more than one ball. (3) Use a light medicine ball.

Games 20 & 21 – Dodge Ball and 3 Court Dodge Ball

Game objective	*Passers* – To hit dodgers below the knee with the ball. *Dodgers* – To avoid being hit with the ball.
Rules	• The ball must not be thrown above waist height. • The ball can be passed among the passers before being thrown at the dodgers. • The dodgers can defend themselves by using their hands to deflect the ball. *In Dodge Ball* – When the dodgers have been hit they : • become passers, or • drop out and watch. *In 3 Court Dodge Ball* – The teams change places when the dodging team has received a total of 3 hits.
Equipment	One large ball.
Organisation	*In Dodge Ball* – Either free running anywhere, or dodgers work within a circle of passers. *In 3 Court Dodge Ball*:

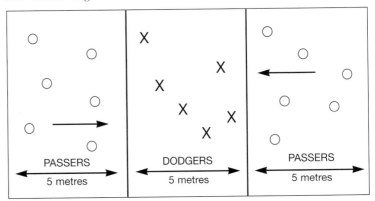

Progression	(1) Increase the number of balls, (2) In 3 Court Dodge Ball increase the number of hits needed before teams change over.

Game 22 – Tower Ball

Game objective	For passers to score by knocking the skittle over.
Rules	• The game starts by a guard passing the ball to a passer. • The passers must stay outside the outer ring. • Guards must stay between the rings. • Teams change over when the skittle has been knocked down three times.
Equipment	2 chalked circles, one large ball, one skittle per game.
Organisation	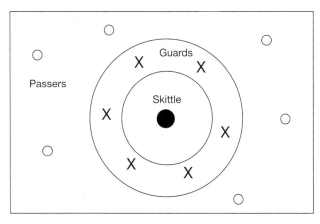
Progression	(1) Increase the number of players. (2) Use a small medicine ball. (3) To Court Tower Ball.

Game 23 – Court Tower Ball

Game objective	To score a goal by knocking over the opposition's skittle.
Rules	• The game starts and restarts with a pass from the centre. • No running with the ball. • No contact. • No player is allowed inside the hoop.
Equipment	Two hoops and one large ball, braids optional.
Organisation	

Game 24 – Crab Football

Game objective	To score a goal.
Rules	• The game is played in the 'crab' position face up with hands and feet on the ground. • Players must keep both hands on the ground. Standing up is NOT permitted. • The game is played by kicking and heading the football. • It is started and restarted by throwing the ball up, between two players, at the centre (as in basketball).
Equipment	Two goals and a large ball.
Organisation	Goals may be marked either by skittles, a gym bench lying on its side or five-a-side football goals.
Progression	Introduce more than one ball.

Game 25 – Zone Ball

Game objective	To score a goal by throwing the ball over the opponent's goal line.
Rules	The game starts with a throw from the centre of the player's own half.
	• The ball must be thrown from where it is retrieved.
	• A bonus of 3-5 steps forward (depending upon the size of the playing area) if the ball is caught.
	• Catching MUST be with two hands.
	• Any type of throw, one handed or two handed, can be allowed, or a specification of the type of throw declared before the game starts.
	• The ball can be caught and thrown from within the end zone.
	• A goal is scored if the ball LANDS in the end zone or crosses the end line.
Equipment	The weight and size of the throwing implement is optional, from bean bag to medicine ball.
	A good variation on this theme is to use hoops, rugby or American footballs, or Pak-Javs.
Organisation	The following dimensions are suitable for older players, but can be increased or decreased according to the age and number of players.

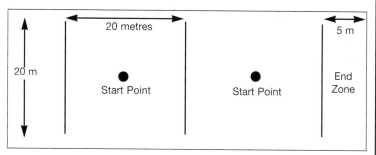

Progression	(1) The coach calls the type of throw to be used as the game progresses.
	(2) A mixture of throwing implements can be used.

SECTION 4 - GAMES INVOLVING CIRCUIT TRAINING

Game 26 – Lucky Spot Circuit Training

Game objective	Involves low impact exercises, to music if wished.
Rules	• The group jog round the centre of the working space while the music plays.
	• When the music is stopped they go and select a Lucky Spot Card.
	• The coach calls out a number.
	• The person with the card of that number goes to the centre and performs the exercise depicted on the card.
	• All join in at the same time.
	The self conscious should work with a partner, or the coach can join them and perform the exercise with them.
Equipment	Lucky Spot Cards, bearing a number, and exercise description, and an exercise illustration.
	A means of playing appropriate background music is optional.
Preparation	Cards are distributed around the periphery of the working area.

Exercise examples

(1)   Burpee.
(2)   Press ups.
(3)   Jumping jacks.
(4)   Star jumps.
(5)   Trunk curls.
(6)   Large arm circles – forwards.
(7)   Large arm circles – backwards.
(8)   Bent leg sit ups.
(9)   Hops on the left leg.
(10) Hops on the right leg.
(11) Raise bent leg in front to hip height one leg at a time.
(12) Raise bent leg behind to opposite hand (low impact).
(13) Double footed low bounces.
(14) Gentle knee bend– rise up on toes.
(15) Marching, swing arms vigorously.
(16) Gentle knee bend – rise up on toes.
(17) Sit and reach - hold for 20 seconds.
(18) Lift alternate legs up and clap hands under the knee.

(19) Twisting hips.
(20) Small arm circles – arms extended at shoulder level.
(21) Alternate arm punches out in front.
(22) Chest expanders– elbows out, then swing wide.
(23) Lower back leg lifts - lie on back and raise opposite hand (low impact).
(24) Walking steps on the spot (low impact).
(25) Calf stretch against the wall – hold for 15 secs.
(26) Setting steps.
(27) Lie on back with knees bent – contract tummy muscles as you breathe out. Breathe in and relax.
(28) Knee lifts (low impact).
(29) Skips.
(30) Gallop steps.
(31) Brisk walking steps.

Game 27 – Odds and Evens Circuit Training

Game objectives	An aerobic circuit of alternate high and low impact exercises lasting 20 minutes. Suitable for the very young with modification.
Rules	• Undertake a general group warm up before starting. • Athletes choose a card from the hoop and find working space. • When all are assembled the coach calls "Begin". They work until the coach calls "Stop!" at the end of one minute. • They return to the hoop and choose another card, move out to do that exercise. • This is repeated for whatever period of time has been chosen. • When completed the group participates in a group warm down.

RED CARDS		BLUE CARDS	
1	Jumping Jack	2	Step Ups
3	Skipping	4	Knee to Elbow
5	Spotty Dogs	6	Race Walking
7	Bench Jumps	8	Jogging
9	Leg Striders	10	Step Kicks
Front	Reverse	Front	Reverse

RECORDING SHEETS

ODDS AND EVENS CIRCUIT		
ACTIVITY	COMPLETED	
ONE		
TWO		
THREE		
FOUR		
FIVE		
SIX		
SEVEN		
EIGHT		
NINE		
TEN		

Equipment	10 pre-prepared work cards bearing five high impact activities on card of one colour, and five low impact activities on card of another colour. One set bear odd numbers on their reverse side, and the other even numbers (see above). 1 hoop and apparatus relative to activities such as skipping ropes, gym mats, benches. Recording sheets and pens or pencils.
Organisation	Place the hoop at the centre of the working area, containing the numbered activity cards. Tell the group that the activities promote heart/lung (cardiovascular) fitness and that each exercise will have to be done for 1 minute. Direct the group to select odd-numbered cards and even-numbered cards alternately. Issue recording sheets and pens/pencils. *Explain/demonstrate the exercises.*
Progression	It is possible to prepare background music so that it signals the one minute working time for each exercise.

RELAY ACTIVITIES

ORGANISATIONAL FORMATS

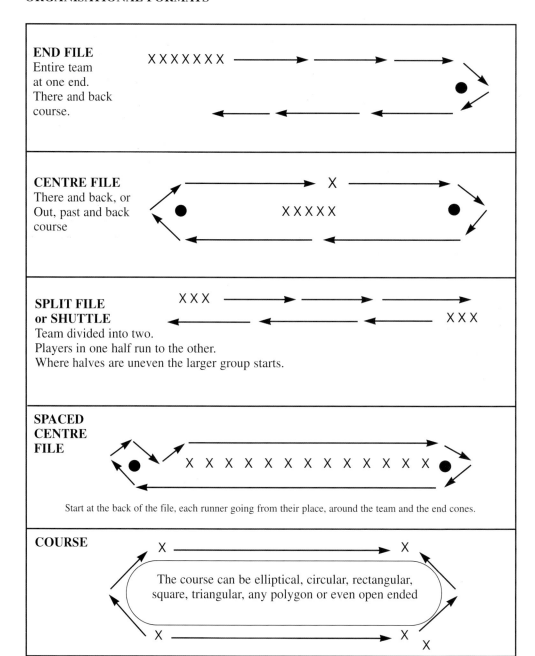

END FILE
Entire team
at one end.
There and back
course.

CENTRE FILE
There and back, or
Out, past and back
course

SPLIT FILE
or SHUTTLE
Team divided into two.
Players in one half run to the other.
Where halves are uneven the larger group starts.

SPACED
CENTRE
FILE

Start at the back of the file, each runner going from their place, around the team and the end cones.

COURSE

The course can be elliptical, circular, rectangular, square, triangular, any polygon or even open ended

CROSSED or COMPASS COURSE

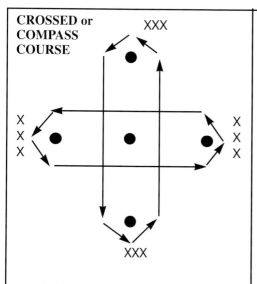

SPRY

Use mostly in throwing relays

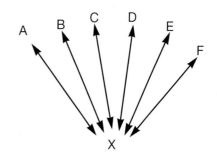

X throws to each of the others in turn, then changes places with A, who eventually changes places with B until all have thrown.

OBJECTIVES or TASKS

Activities
1. Make runs in team order.
2. Entire team run together (stream).
3. Carry out a given task.
4. Carry out a given task and run.
5. Team carry out a set task.
6. Team carry out a set task and run.

Duration
1. To a total per person.
2. To a team total.
3. For a set time.
4. To a total PLUS a time.

FURTHER RELAY ACTIVITY IDEAS

SHUTTLE RELAYS

There are many variants of Shuttle relays requirng no equipment other than a relay baton. Even this is not essential. Most use the SPLIT FILE format, although END FILE is better when space is limited. CENTRE FILE permits a baton passing technique similar to that used in the 'proper' outdoor form to be used and practised. SHUTTLE relays can involve each athlete only running once, or be CONTINUOUS so that each makes several runs. A LINEAR Shuttle relay can also be a combination of CENTRE FILE and SPLIT FILE formats.

CONTINUOUS RELAYS

As the title suggests these continue until one of the four duration objectives or tasks is fulfilled. A single repetition relay is a continuous relay in which each runner makes only one run. **N.B.** CONTINUOUS COURSE relays always need ONE athlete MORE in each team than the number of legs to be run in the relay.

COMBINATION RELAYS

This format involves more than one activity in the competition. They are usually organised in the END FILE mode, although it is possible to use any of the other formats.

SPRINTING & HURDLING RELAYS

Format – SPLIT or END file, and CONTINUOUS or SINGLE.

e.g. Hurdle Relays

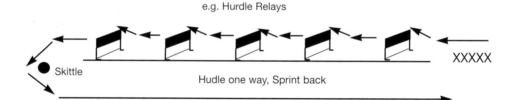

Skittle

Hudle one way, Sprint back

XXXXX

Rules

- Each runner returns to the *back* of the file, and
- there is no change-over contact (the outgoing runner starts when the incoming runner passes the hurdle nearest to the start).

Progressions

(1) Add another lane of hurdles facing in the opposite direction so that runners can hurdle going in both directions.
(2) Sprint first, and hurdle back.
(3) Hop, or double-foot jump over the hurdles then sprint back.
(4) Hurdle going out, and hop or double-foot jump returning.
(5) Leave out hurdles and:
   - hop in one direction and sprint back, or
   - hop out on the right leg, and back on the left leg, or
   - hop out and double-foot jump back, or
   - any combination of hopping, double-foot jumping and running.

WEAVING RELAY
Format – SPACED CENTRE FILE

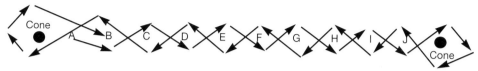

Rules
- Athlete **A** runs, weaving out and back, and circling both cones.
- **A** hands over by touching **B** and sits down in his/her own place.
- When **D** runs he/she must still weave between **A, B**, and **C** in both directions.
- Players may be either seated, standing or alternately seated and standing for this relay.

OVER THE LEGS
Format - SPACED CENTRE FILE

Rules
- Two teams sit facing each other, with legs outstretched and feet touching (teams need to be numerically balanced).
- Runners race over the legs, round the cones, and back behind their team.
- The next runner starts when the previous runner sits down.

SPACED CENTRE FILE RELAYS
CENTRE FILE RELAYS from a standing, or sitting start provide a further variation to the relay theme, and can incorporate a wealth of differing activities. These may include hopping, double-foot jumps, carrying objects such as medicine balls or even fellow team members.

OVER AND UNDER

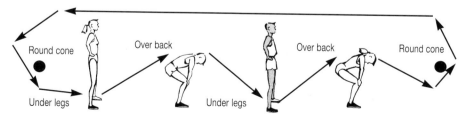

Smaller or younger participants crouch to make the back for leap-frog since they may not have the strength, or ability to leap-frog someone standing up. The player making the back may also not be strong enough to support another child.

Progressions
Leap-frog in which ALL players make a back and vault over each other in turn.

OVER AND UNDER BALL PASSING

Rules
- When the last player in the line receives the ball he/she runs with it to the front and the whole team shuffles back one place.
- The relay finishes when the player who started at the front of the team is back in their starting position.

Progressions
(1) When the last player receives the ball the entire team turns round and the ball is passed back in the opposite direction. The relay continues for a set number of 'lengths'.

(2) Cones are placed at either end of the team, and the player carrying the ball to the front of the team has to go around the cones and the team, before going to the front of the team and recommencing the passing.

(3) The entire team falls in behind the runner carrying the ball after he/she passes the front position and follows them around the cones back into position ready to recommence passing.

BENCH PASSING RELAY

Rules
- The teams stands astride a gym bench.
- They pick it up together and hold it between their legs.
- The bench is passed forwards using hands only.
- When there is no longer any bench to hold each last player runs to the front of the team, steps astride the protruding portion, takes hold of it and continues passing it forwards.
- Players must NOT move forwards when holding the bench.

The relay finishes either:
- when each player has returned to their starting place, or
- when the bench has been moved a predetermined distance.

TASK RELAY
Format - END FILE, CENTRE FILE or COURSE.

This type of relay can be given a CONDITIONING or SKILL focus. There are numerous variants. Determining factors include the training effect desired, the facilities that are available, and the age of the participants.

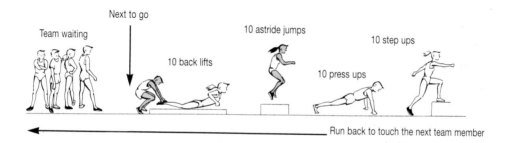

Coaches will need to keep a careful watch on all tasks to ensure that:
- all are correctly performed, and that
- the specified number of repetitions are completed.

OBSTACLE RELAY
This involves running and moving 'over and under' or 'around' and 'through' items of apparatus - as in the television programme – Gladiators. The variety of constructions is limited only by the imagination and ingenuity of the coach. At all times, however. activities must be safe.

SKINNING the SNAKE
Format - CENTRE FILE.

Teams stand side on with hands joined. They step over the RIGHT hand with the RIGHT leg and retain the hold. This brings them into a position in which they now face the front holding joined hands between their legs.

Rules
- The whole team shuffles backwards, holding hands.
- Each player lies down in turn and lets the others shuffle over them, starting with the rear one, until they are all lying on their backs with hands joined.

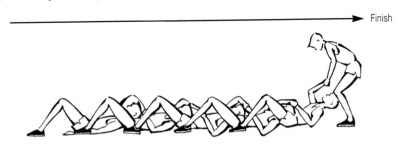

This is a superb activity as the last of a series of consecutive relays.

BUNNIES RELAY
Format – END FILE or CENTRE FILE.

Rules
- The team squats in a line holding onto the hips of the player in front.
- The front player stands facing the team holding the hands of the next player.
- He/she walks backwards and the team follow doing Bunny jumps, and retaining their hold on the player in front of them.
- When they reach the end of the course all run back to finish at the starting point.

CAUTION: This is hard on the knees so don't overdo it!

COURSE RELAYS

TICK, or TAG RELAY

Organisation
A 100m circular course needs to be constructed. It will have a 15.76m radius.
5 teams can be accommodated at 20m intervals, or 4 at 25m intervals, or 3 at 33m intervals.

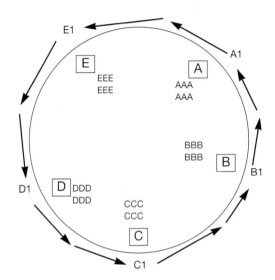

Rules
- Teams sit in file inside the circle facing out.
- Each member runs one lap before passing on to the next.
- The chase continues until one team catches that in front and touches, 'ticks' or 'tags' them.
- The chase stops.
- Both teams involved in the 'tick'/'tag' change places and resume the chase.
- Each 'tick'/'tag' scores one point for the team making it.

Equipment
Measuring tape for construction of the circle and cones to mark it out. Relay batons are optional.

Progressions
The course shape can be changed, it doesn't have to be circular.

PURSUIT RELAY

Organisation
The course is essentially the same as that used for the Tick Relay and like it need not be circular.

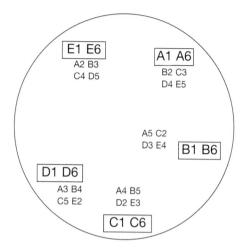

Rules
- Team members are distributed around each of the change-over stations (there are 5 teams of 6 runners in the example).
- Only the first and last runners (1 & 6) in each team occupy the same station.
- Each team starts from a different point.
- Each player runs to the next change-over station and hands over to the next in their team.
- The contest continues until each runner has returned to the point from which they started.

Equipment
As for 'Tick' or 'Tag' relay.
Each 'tick'/'tag' scores one point for the team making it.

CONTINUOUS RELAY

This example utilises a 400m track, but this type of relay is possible on any shape of course. This particular example involves 8 stages, or 'legs' to be run, and thus requires 9 runners to each team.

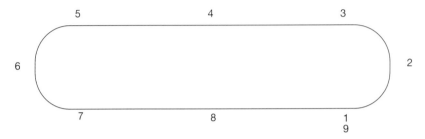

Rules

- Each runner covers 50m, and remains at the change-over station until it is their turn to run again.
- The 9th runner runs the same 'leg' as the first and provides the vital link between 8th and 1st to achieve continuity.

The race continues for either a predetermined number of laps, or for a set time.

PAARLAUF

This is a special form of continuous relay popular with Senior endurance runners

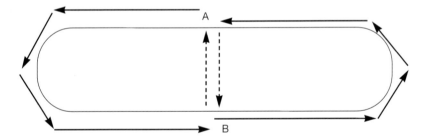

Rules

- The original format involves only 2 runners per team.
- The race begins at the middle of a straight.
- Each runner covers 200m.
- After each change-over the incoming runner jogs across the infield to meet up with his/her partner where they began their run.

The race is for a pre-set number of laps. or for a pre-set time.

Progressions

For younger athletes increase team size to three or more.

CROSS COUNTRY RELAYS

Cross Country running can be made more interesting and enjoyable for young athletes by turning the run into a large Continuous relay over a course of irregular shape, and with 'legs' of varying lengths.

HARE and HOUNDS RUNS

Hare and Hounds is a special team game devised to make Cross Country and Road Running attractive to young athletes.

Game objective

(a) For the Hounds – to run the course as fast as possible, and to catch as many Hares as possible.

(b) For the Hares – to run the course as fast as possible, and to stay ahead of the Hounds.

Rules

- The competing teams need to be of approximately the same size and ability.
- A familiar course should be used.
- One team is designated Hares and the other Hounds.
- The Hares set off a short time before the Hounds.
- The result is decided in the opposite way to a normal Cross Country race. The winner is awarded the same number of points as there are Hounds PLUS a bonus of two points for each Hare passed.
- The Hares do not score but must still run the course.

On subsequent occasions when the competition is run, a different team are given the task of being Hares until all have done so. When this has been completed scores can be matched and a winning team found.

Example
Organisation for four teams running Hare and Hounds once per week for 4 weeks.

Date	WEEK1	WEEK 2	WEEK 3	WEEK 4
TEAM A	Hares			
TEAM B		Hares		
TEAM C			Hares	
TEAM D				Hares
TOTAL				

EVENT SPECIFIC GAMES

These are to be found in the sections devoted to the Running and Jumping event groups where relevant special games are appropriate.

POTTED SPORTS

A POTTED SPORTS or DYNAMIC ATHLETICS MEETING is a team competition in which teams attempt a variety of events or activities in a course sequence. These may be traditional athletic events, or modified, non-traditional ones, or a mixture of both. Performance standards can be pre-set. The objective is for members of the team to perform as well as possible at each activity, recording either their best performance, or the best standard attained, or the total of all their attempts. These go toward the team total at the end of the course. When the competition is based on the total of all of each competitor's attempts there is a large endurance factor and the activities selected should not demand high levels of skill.

EVENTS

The skill requirement should be such that the activity can be repeated, and technique will not markedly deteriorate as fatigue increases. The events should incorporate skills that have already been experienced, and which are also *safe*.

STANDARDS

For most events a number of target standards - usually three – can be set. The lowest standard should be such that *all* participants are capable of attaining it. The middle standard should be within the scope of most, whilst only a few should be capable of the hardest one. A close knowledge of the abilities of all in the group will enable the coach to set standards which challenge all, and pack each activity with interest. A means of recording results is necessary, so that individuals can assess progress, and be motivated by it, if it is intended to repeat the session.

PROCEDURE

1. Each team requires a parent, or non-competing leader, to be scorer.
2. Each team commences the competition at a different activity.
3. Teams work at each activity for a specified time (2 to 5 minutes) depending on the age of the athletes.
4. There needs to be a rest interval between activities during which scores can be calculated and recorded before the team moves on to the next event.
5. All participants take part in each activity, in strict rotation.
6. Individuals are permitted as many attempts as possible within the time set.
7. It is useful to keep a running score so that it can be announced at each change of activities (see sample results sheet).

SCORING

Several options are open which can focus upon either the BEST or the TOTAL:

	BEST	**TOTAL**
Individual scores	Use only the BEST of all attempts made at each activity in the time set.	Use ALL of the attempts made at each activity in the time set.
TEAM SCORES	Add up the BEST attempts of each team member.	Add up the TOTAL scores of each team member.

Individual and team competitions can be decided upon the total score, or scores can be recognised and recorded separately for each event, in which case there can be several 'winners'. Competitions in which standards are set score 1 point for attaining the lowest standard, 2 points for the next, 3 for the next, and so on. For Shuttle Runs 1 point is scored for each run/lap completed, by each runner, in the time set. They can be organised as a relay in which each runner goes individually, or as a steady 'team' run in which the whole team runs together.

ORGANISATIONAL OPTIONS
1. Teams do the SAME EVENTS SIMULTANEOUSLY – this works well with younger children, especially indoors using simple activities. It has the advantage that team positions are known to all throughout the competition.
2. BEST SCORE TOTALS with STANDARDS – has the disadvantage that the good performer who attains the highest standard on the first attempt then has nothing to strive for.
3. Use a RELAY TO SET THE WORKING TIME FOR ALL TEAMS – this means that the quicker the relay is run the less time the other teams have to accumulate a high score.

SAMPLE RESULT SHEET
This should be drawn up on a large board (black or white board) or on an OHP before the competition commences and filled in as the competition progresses. Place the score for each event above the diagonal dividing each rectangle, and the running score below it.

TEAMS	EVENT						Results	
	STANDING LONG JUMP	MED. BALL for HEIGHT	SHUTTLE RELAY	STANDING TRIPLE JUMP	MED. BALL CHEST PUT	BKD ROLL to HANDSTAND	POINTS TOTAL	POS.
Team A								
Team B								
Team C								
Team D								

EXAMPLES OF POTTED SPORTS FORMATS

A. Indoors

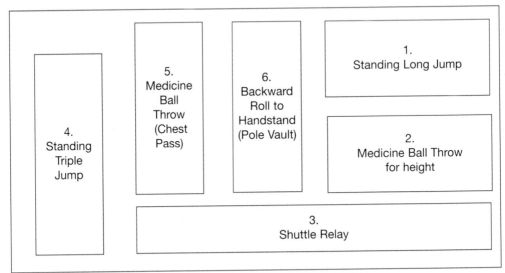

Fig. P1

Explanation of events for Indoor example A:

1.	STANDING LONG JUMP	TWO foot take off to TWO foot landing.
2.	MEDICINE BALL THROW for HEIGHT	Small medicine ball thrown over an elastic high jump bar. NO CATCHING.
3.	SHUTTLE RELAY	Score for each run made.
4.	STANDING TRIPLE JUMP	ONE foot to SAME foot, to OTHER foot, to BOTH feet
5.	MEDICINE BALL CHEST PUT	Standing TWO handed push from chest.
6.	BACKWARD ROLL to HANDSTAND	Backward roll to clear elastic high jump bar set at a height of 30cms.

B. Indoors

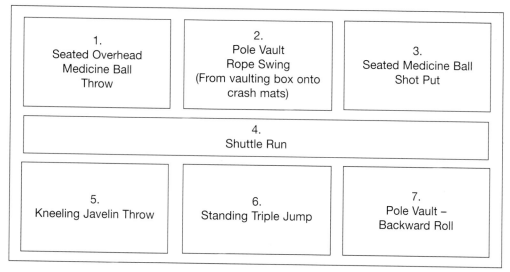

1. Seated Overhead Medicine Ball Throw	2. Pole Vault Rope Swing (From vaulting box onto crash mats)	3. Seated Medicine Ball Shot Put
4. Shuttle Run		
5. Kneeling Javelin Throw	6. Standing Triple Jump	7. Pole Vault – Backward Roll

Fig. P2

Explanation of events for Indoor example B:

1.	SEATED BALL THROW	Swing from 2 or 3 sections of a vaulting box onto crash mats at the same height.
3.	SEATED MEDICINE BALL CHEST PUT	Seated single hand put from chest.
4.	TEAM SHUTTLE RUN	The whole team runs together.
5.	KNEELING 'JAVELIN' THROW	Kneeling version of activity 1.
6.	STANDING THREE SPRING JUMPS	3 successive TWO foot to TWO foot jumps.
7.	STANDING HIGH JUMP	Standing High Jump using Tip-2-Tip vertical jump measurer.

C. Outdoors (using a Playing Field)

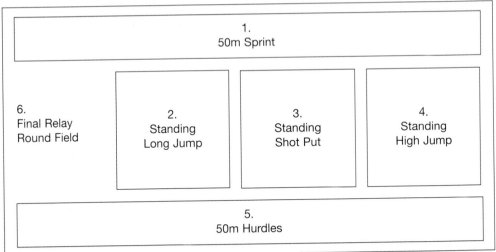

Fig. P3

Explanation of events for Outdoor example C

1.	50m SPRINT	All team members run once - three pre-set time standards
2.	STANDING LONG JUMP	ONE foot take off and TWO foot landing.
3.	STANDING SHOT PUT	Thrower retrieves own shot - more than one shot in use so that there is no need to pass from one person to another.
4.	STANDING HIGH JUMP	Over elastic bar - score 2 points for every clearance.
5.	50m HURDLES	As for 50m sprint above.
6.	RELAY AROUND FIELD	As a final event in which all teams compete together.

D. Outdoors (using a Track)

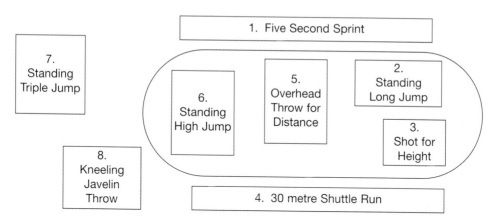

Fig. P 4

Explanation of events for Outdoor example D

1.	5 SECOND SPRINT	All team members get one turn - standards are distances to be reached in 5 seconds.
2.	SIX STRIDE LONG JUMP	Run 6 strides and jump - measure from point of take-off - a spotter is needed.
3.	SHOT THROW for HEIGHT	Use a medicine ball or football with younger competitors.
4.	SHUTTLE RUN	As above.
5.	BACKWARDS OVERHEAD THROW	A TWO handed throw with back to the landing area.
6.	TWO STRIDE HIGH JUMP	High jump from TWO stride approach.
7.	STANDING TWO HOPS, TWO STEPS, TWO JUMPS	SAME - SAME - OTHER - OTHER - TOGETHER - TOGETHER.
8.	KNEELING JAVELIN THROW	Use TWO hands to throw either a small javelin or football.

Special measuring mats for jumping can be obtained. Failing that a measuring tape and chalked heels works wonderfully when sand pits are not available.

These examples are not the only Potted Sports formats.

DEVISE YOU OWN VERSION FOR YOUR OWN SPECIAL NEEDS

CONDITIONING

WHAT

Conditioning is a physical thing and involves 'GETTING FIT TO TRAIN'. There are five basic elements of training, and because each begins with the letter 'S' they are generally referred to as the FIVE Ss. In the triangular model below, Suppleness, Stamina and Strength underpin Skill and Speed.

SPEED
SKILL
STRENGTH
STAMINA
SUPPLENESS

In an alternative, equally correct model they follow each other in this order . . .

SUPPLENESS > SKILL > SPEED > STAMINA > STRENGTH . . .

because suppleness is of first importance, particularly when the athletes are very young, or first starting, then skill (particularly through the 'skill hungry years') then speed and so on. As in all forms of athletic preparation, Conditioning should progress from the General to the Specific.

GENERAL CONDITIONING, which involves 'getting fit to train', comes first. It establishes the bases of Suppleness, Stamina and Strength, so that further work can be accomplished covering ALL aspects of the FIVE Ss.

SPECIFIC CONDITIONING follows, and embraces the development of those aspects of fitness which are specific, or peculiar to the event for which the athlete is training. This training is frequently skill related, and thus blends in with skill development.

WHY

Conditioning is necessary in order to provide a foundation upon which further specific work can be built. A well conditioned athlete will ultimately be able to train harder, recover quicker, and be less susceptible to injury than one who is less well prepared.

WHEN

Conditioning commences at the beginning (Phase 1) of each year's training, that is during the months October to December. The length and nature of the training carried out at this time will depend upon:-

The EVENT
The AGE of the Athlete
The FITNESS of the Athlete
The STRENGTHS and WEAKNESS of the Athlete.

General conditioning will play a large part in the training undertaken by each athlete at the beginning of their career. The relationship between the volume and intensity of this work needs to be carefully balanced throughout, so that the end product bears no weaknesses which may hinder later development. A further important training principle, that of Specificity, dictates that the nature of the event determines the degree by which each of the Five-Ss plays a part in the preparation of the refined product. Conditioning thus has an integral part to play in the early training programme of a young athlete, but must not assume greater importance than enjoyment and the establishment of a sound skills foundation.

HOW
(a) **Suppleness**
If mobility exercises are neglected the outermost range of movement will diminish. During infancy and childhood this range is at its optimum, but can begin to deteriorate as early as age eight. Special mobility training sessions should be part of the training programme. Their purpose should be firstly to ascertain the outer ranges of movement possessed by each athlete, and then to improve upon them, as far as needed in order to perform the skills of the event effectively. Once the required levels have been established then the purpose of mobility training changes to one of maintenance. It is important to convince young athletes of the need for these exercises, and of their importance to training. Once they become sufficiently motivated about them to do them regularly at home, on their own then the battle has been won.

(b) **Stamina**
The improvement and maintenance of general levels of endurance is important to most athletes, and certainly to all young athletes. Greatest attention is ascribed to aerobic endurance at the beginnings of training - training life and the training year. The amount of work undertaken will need to relate to the requirements of the athlete and of the event. It is important to bear in mind that there are many more routes to aerobic improvement than simply running long distances at a steady pace. For some athletes this may be the worst possible route. Other methods are:-

Fartlek
Paarlauf
Continuous relays
Interval running
Circuit training, or from outside athletics

Cycling
Swimming, and
Team games.

For details of each refer to the Endurance Running, Relays, and Circuit Training sections of this booklet.

(c) **Strength**
The most effective way to improve strength is to use barbells or dumbbells. This route is not suitable for young athletes because their bones are immature, and may not be appropriate to some events. The sport generally advises against the introduction of weight training into the conditioning programme until the participant's skeleton is reasonably mature, i.e. the athlete is competing in the Under 17 age group. Only in instances in which the coach is very experienced in weight training, and has strong influence and control over his charges, should work with weights be part of the training programme of athletes younger than this.

During early years strength improvement should be sought using the athlete's own body-weight using exercises like the examples given on pages 15, 16 and 44-49. The most effective way of organising this work is in CIRCUIT TRAINING, see pages 40-41. Other, more specific, ways of developing strength include:-

Hill running – running strong, short intervals up hills
Resistance running – in a harness running against which a partner
places a resistance, and

Plyometric Training

Rebound training of this type develops Elastic Strength. It requires the subject to have already pre-conditioned the legs and back in a general way before embarking on this special programme. Its more common format employs various jumping activities, although the principle can be applied to torso and upper limbs using medicine balls, particularly if they are first caught before being thrown back to a 'deliverer'. Easy loadings, involving heights jumped over, and from, and light medicine balls, as well as the total number of repetitions completed, ought to be the order of the day when introducing them to beginners. Progression to more strenuous work should be very gradual.

Careful, caring introduction of these activities to the young is a necessary precursor to the successful employment of such training techniques by some groups of adult athletes, e.g. throwers.

PUTTING CONDITIONING and REGENERATION into
THE TRAINING CONTINUUM.

Examples are given of a typical emphasis appropriate to an adult athlete which can be compared with one more applicable to a young athlete of secondary school age.

(a)   A training year for a Senior Athlete having a major peak in August/September.

	Oct	Nov	Dec	Jan	Feb	Mar	Apr	May	Jun	Jul	Aug	Sept
Phase of Training	6	1	1	1	2	2	3	3	3	4	5	5
Conditioning		General	General	General	Specific	Specific				Specific		
Recovery	X			x			x		x		x	
Application							x	x	x		x	**X**

N.B. The numbers against Phases of Training indicate:-
1.   PREPARATION – Phase 1 – starting easy and gradually increasing the quantity of work output.
2.   PREPARATION – Phase II – in which the quality of the work increases gradually to competition levels.
3.   COMPETITION – Phase I – in which weekly workload is reduced in order to have something in reserve for the weekend competition.
4.   COMPETITION – Phase II – during which weekly training reverts to the levels of Preparation Phase II and competition is accorded lesser status.
5.   COMPETITION – Phase III – in which the athlete returns to work/competition emphases like those in Competition Phase 1.
6.   TRANSITION or RECOVERY – in which a 'holiday' is taken from competition and training.

(b)   A training year for a School Age Athlete having a major peak in July.

	Oct	Nov	Dec	Jan	Feb	Mar	Apr	May	Jun	Jul	Aug	Sept
Phase	6	1	1	1	2	2	3	3	3	5	3	3
Conditioning		General	General	General	Specific	Specific					Specific	
Recovery	**X**			x			x				x	
Application							x	x	x	**X**	x	x

These tables afford a general indication of the timing and type of conditioning appropriate to each. Detailed refinement is needed to meet the particular requirements of individual athletes and specific competition programmes.

SUMMARY

1.   GENERAL CONDITIONING is done during Preparation – Phase 1 of training, and at the beginning of the athlete's career.
2.   SPECIFIC CONDITIONING follows General Conditioning.
3.   Conditioning is essential to the athletes future, particularly if it is to be competitively successful.
4.   Start conditioning with very light or low loads, and progress gradually.
5.   REGENERATION or RECOVERY is as important as training, particularly for the young. It should be fitted in to the programme wherever, or whenever necessary. As a simple guide – a short period of regeneration should be planned whenever the emphasis of training changes.
6.   BEYOND THAT it is prudent to programme Rest into each week of training, in addition to each session of training. At least three midweek days off, plus one at the weekend is a sound recipe for younger athletes.

FURTHER READING

The following BAF publications, written by experienced
National Athletics Coaches, will prove invaluable to teachers
and coaches who introduce athletics activities to youngsters
in a class or group situation:

HOW TO TEACH THE JUMPS by David Lease

HOW TO TEACH THE THROWS by Carl Johnson

HOW TO TEACH TRACK EVENTS by Malcolm Arnold

and the comprehensive BUT FIRST by Frank Dick

For details contact:
B.A.F. Athletics Bookcentre
5 Church Road, Great Bookham,
Surrey KT23 3PN

Tel: (01372) 452804

EVENTS IN GROUPS

RUNNING

BASIC PRINCIPLES
Running is without doubt the most popular athletic activity. It has three main divisions:
- Sprinting
- Endurance
- Hurdling.

SPRINTING involves running fast, up to distances of 400m, and includes Relays which are team events generally, but not necessarily, involving four runners who combine their efforts in covering a set distance. The standard adult events are 4 x 100m and 4 x 400m.

ENDURANCE includes those events in which running is sustained over distances greater than those which can be sprinted. It is sub-divided as follows:
- Middle Distance (800m and 1500m)
- Long Distance (3000m, 5000m and 10,000m)
- Road Running takes place over similar distances to the Long Endurance events, going up to Marathon (26miles 385yds, or 42.195km) and even beyond
- Cross Country Running (a winter activity)
- Steeplechase, a track race in which solid barriers and a water jump have to be cleared, and
- Fell/Hill Running (a high terrain activity)

The division also embraces Race Walking which is not really a running event but one in which the distances raced make them endurance activities.

HURDLING involves sprinting over a series of 7 to 10 obstacles, depending upon age, light enough to be knocked over if struck by the runner.

PRIMARY RUNNING ACTIVITIES
These are for the very young performer. They are PRIMARY because they are FIRST activities and are appropriate to those in PRIMARY SCHOOLS, and of PRIMARY SCHOOL age, particularly the 8s to 11s.

At this age 'Discovery' methods, or 'Learning through Experience' are popular teaching formats in the educational world. They are equally appropriate out of school, in clubs or in local authority recreation programmes. This way of working involves setting the performer(s) a Task, or a Challenge, as a result of which a deduction, or deductions can be made, and by which the child, or children establish rules, or principles of work, or movement. In the Physical Education world it is commonly referred to as Movement Education

Such tasks for running may include:	They are presented in groups which address:
• run on the spot (or in place) • run forwards • run backwards • run sideways • run in a clockwise circle • run in an anti-clockwise circle • run a zigzag course	• balance, and • placement of body-weight
• run heavily • run noisily • run lightly • run quietly	• quality and mode of ground contact
• run lifting your knees to hip height • run kicking your bottom with your heels	• popular skill drills
• run with your arms folded across your chest • run holding a stick or relay baton in front	• use of the arms
• run in slow motion • run quickly • run as fast as you can • run at varying speeds	• speed
• run varying distances • run varying distances at a set pace • run for varying lengths of time	• sustained running and pace judgement
• run freely around, or between scattered objects • run around, or between objects placed in a particular pattern – these may eventually simulate a running track	• running around a course
• run with a partner • run in step with a partner • run in step with a partner; then one of you increases the length of their strides – what happens? • run in step with a partner; then one of you quickens their steps – what happens?	• co-operation in running • stride length and frequency

• run in groups following a course set by a leader – change leaders frequently • run in single file, while each back person runs quickly to the front	• co-operation in running • stride length and frequency
• run as far as you can in 6 secs, or 8 secs, or 10 secs – mark where you get to and try again • run as far as you can in 2 mins; or 5 mins, or 10 mins or even 15 mins – a course is needed and the number of laps completed recorded.	• sustained running and pace judgement

Complemented by frequent, sensible, pertinent questioning this work will make children aware of the results of running in particular ways, and of those ways which are most effective. Appropriate questioning will lead towards deductions as to the most effective ways in which to run fast, or for a length of time, and to the establishment of a set of basic principles which can be applied to most running challenges.

SPRINTING

THE BASIC MODEL

Keep to basic principles but remain aware of the fact that each young sprinter has the potential to develop into a very accomplished adult performer, if not an Olympic champion. Young Linford Christies need to be given the chance to realise their full potential, rather than be coached into poor imitations of Steve Cram.

The use of special sprint drills is now commonplace in most sprint groups, whatever their age or ability. The sprints coach, however, has to be very clear in his own mind as to:

- Why the drills are being performed.
- Whether they are drills being performed correctly
- Whether the athletes are learning from what they are doing

Drills are frequently delivered and performed in an unthinking way: more for the sake of copying what others do than to gain, or learn anything positive, from the exercise. It is the duty of the coach to ensure that this does not happen.

Drills are generally utilised as precursors to the main training session, as an active link between warm-up and hard exercise. This is an important time for observation and instruction. Bad habits, detrimental to advanced development, can be too easily learned as the result of unchecked, and uncorrected work.

A good way of doing this type of work is to set a task in which the performer is required to focus upon a particular aspect of technique during each performance. Such tasks may include running:

- strongly
- tall (with high hips), and/or
- lightly . . .
- on the balls of the feet
- with knees high in front
- and keeping the body upright (shoulders pressed forwards a little)
- without sitting
- keeping shoulders low, and
- maintaining bent arms (concentrating upon the elbows)
- keeping head still (focus ahead).

When this format is repeated session after session slowly but surely technical correctness starts to be established and become an integral part of the running habit.

DEVELOPMENT

The individual technical focus needs to be upon:-

(a) the arms.
(b) the legs, and
(c) complementary activity by other body parts

within the concept of the Basic Model of Sprinting.

The matter of how much drilling, and how often is an important one. Whilst the very young sprinter will benefit from doing most sprint drills, it must be borne in mind that doing sprint drills to the exclusion of all else, can be detrimental to the establishment of good sprinting technique.

The 'Learning by Experience' approach will take the child through activities in which:
- running heavily: is contrasted with running lightly
- running on the heels: is contrasted with running on the balls of the feet
- running with long strides: is contrasted with running with short strides
- running with slow steps: is contrasted with running with quick ones,
- running with high knees:is contrasted with kicking one's heels to one's bottom, and
- running tall: is contrasted with running bunched up.

These contrasts lead children to correct deductions as to what is right and wrong in the process of establishing effective principles of running.

Children of about 12 years of age can handle repeated runs over 30 to 40 metres at an easy striding speed in which the action of a different body part is emphasised, such as:-

(a) HEAD
- "Keep your eyes looking directly forward".
- "Focus on something in the distance".
- "Keep the top of your head up - but NOT the forehead".

(b) SHOULDERS
- "Do not let them roll".
- "Do not lift them up".
- "Keep them low and still".
- "Shrug them to your ears, and then push them down".

(c) ARMS
- "Let them do the running".
- "Keep them close to your body".

(d) HIPS
- "Do not sit".
- "Do not lift the shoulders when the hips are lifted (this is not easy)"

(e) LEGS
- "Run on the balls of the feet"
- "High knees are important – they should come up to hip height but no higher.

To summarise – run tall, lightly, and with good knee lift whilst thinking about looking straight ahead, and keeping hips high and shoulders low.

DRILLS
(1) The HIGH KNEES drill (fig R1) involves picking the knees to hip height in front of the body, but no higher than hip height, or this will encourage sitting.
(2) BACK KICKS (fig R2) in which the runners heels are flicked backwards to touch the buttocks are useful for keeping the quadriceps supple, and for toning the hamstrings. They are also supposed to rehearse the folding action of the leg during its recovery and thereby contribute to leg speed. Performers must stay on their toes, and keep the arms moving throughout.

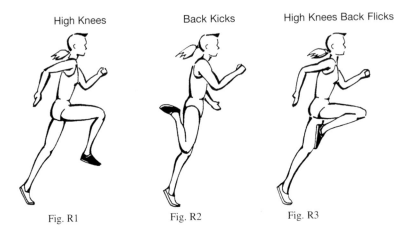

High Knees   Back Kicks   High Knees Back Flicks

Fig. R1   Fig. R2   Fig. R3

(3)   HIGH KNEE BACK FLICKS (fig R3) are a combination of the previous two drills, and as a total exercise perhaps closest to the sprinting action. The action involves lifting the knee to hip height whilst simultaneously flicking the heel backwards to make contact with the upper hamstrings (it is not possible to get to the buttocks in this drill).

(4)   FOR ARMS – particularly to correct an action in which they move across the body instead of forwards and backwards.

Get the runners to carry a stick, relay baton, golf ball or stone in each hand. This heightens consciousness of what they are doing. The elbows need to remain close by the side, whilst the hands swing to shoulder height ahead of the body, and the elbows to shoulder height behind – high elbows to the rear – high knees in front, and vice-versa.

It is best to commence these drills working 'on the spot' or 'in place' in order to groove the correct technique before changing to the moving mode. They are then practised over a total distance of 20 metres – the first 10 metres being covered slowly, while concentrating on good form, then speeding up over the last 10 and endeavouring to hold that form.

Further drills can involve:

(a)   Starting slowly and building up speed until the legs are moving as fast as they can.

(b)   Placing three equally spaced markers on the track (e.g. each 10 metres apart) then running fast to the first mark, easing off slightly to the second, and finishing fast to the third.

When each individual run has been completed the runner walks slowly back to the start in order to recover sufficiently before beginning the next run.

STARTING

1. STANDING STARTS

Standing starts are for the very young because they are not sufficiently strong or diligent enough to be able to derive benefit from a Crouch Start.

How to do, and teach them. . .
- walk to the Start Line, and
- stand with the preferred foot just behind it, and the other foot back behind that.

If necessary let the runners experiment using both feet as the front one, in turn, until they arrive at some sort of preference.

Key points:
  • Body-weight should act through the front leg.

On the command "Set" . . .
  • The hips are lowered by bending both legs slightly, while
  • the arms are placed so that they oppose the position of the legs (right arm forward if the left leg is forward, and vice versa).

On "Go". . .
  • Drive away strongly.

2. 'FALL' STARTS

These provide an effective way of inculcating some of the qualities required of the Crouch Start before it is actually learned, or needed. It is thus a most appropriate developmental activity for young athletes.
  How to do, and teach them . . .
  • Stand behind the Start Line with both feet together.
  • Lean, and fall forwards, like a felled tree.
  • Drive away strongly, but
  • stay low as this push is made.
  • Keep the head low to encourage other body parts to remain low.

3.   CROUCH STARTS

Demonstrate a Crouch Start, and get the children to copy. They will already have decided which foot they prefer to place forward as the result of their previous experiences. How to do this, and teach them . . .
  • measure 1½ foot lengths back from the Start Line.
  • stand with the front foot on this mark, and
  • sink to kneel on the other knee, which is placed in line with the ankle of the front foot.
  The standard "On your Marks" position is then completed by:
  • placing the hands behind the Start Line so that they are:

Fig. R4

Fig. R5

71

(a) shoulder width apart;
(b) the fingers pointing outwards, and the thumb inwards, whilst
(c) a high bridge is formed between the fingers and thumbs.
   • The shoulders should be directly over the hands, and
   • the head must remain looking down.

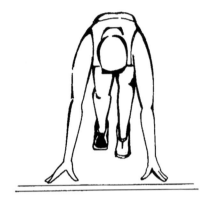

Fig. R6   Fig. R7

On the command "Set" . . .
   • the hips are raised to a position a little higher than the shoulders.
This should not happen too quickly, otherwise they will have to support themselves on their fingers for a long time, and balance will be lost.
   On "Go" . . .
   • the runners drive forwards and into their running.
The 'key' here is *forwards*. Most youngsters make the mistake of standing up first, and then beginning to run. The key instructional point is thus:
   • stay low, and come up gradually.
The runners can imagine that they are starting in a low tunnel which gradually gets higher. If the head is lifted too soon – the roof awaits! Get a partner to stand 2 to 3 metres away, and stretch out an arm to simulate the tunnel roof, so that the runner can concentrate upon driving under it.

FURTHER HELPFUL STARTING ACTIVITIES

(a)   10 STRIDE RUNS
Participants work in pairs, one running while the other 'spots' and marks. The runner starts, and drives out as hard as possible. The 'spotter' counts, and places a marker on the spot where the 10th stride lands. The spotter and runner then change places, and roles. A distinctive marker is needed for the second runner. Each make several runs, and try to extend their mark by driving harder on each run.

(b) STARTS FROM SIDE-ON SITTING

These give runners experience of moving forwards into their running, and of coming up gradually from a low position. They closely resemble the movements required of a good start from the crouch position, and are fun to do. Runners sit facing at right angles to the line of run. They turn and run in one continuous action on the starting command.

(c) PRONE STARTS

Fig. R8

The runners adopt the prone position with head at the Start Line (fig. R8). They push up and run on the command. Such starts provide further experience of running forward and out from the start while staying low. Fast feet, as they move forward under the body, are important.

(d) REACTION STARTS

These provide practice in reacting quickly to the starting command, and thus offer important experiences for budding sprinters.
Suitable activities include:
  • "Who can move first"?
  • "Who can get to a pre-arranged mark (15 metres) first"?
  They can take place from a variety of starting positions. In addition to (b) and (c) above they can include:
  • Lying supine with feet nearer the Start Line (fig. R9).
  • Lying supine with head nearer the Start Line.

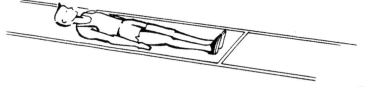

Fig. R9

Activities (b), (c) and (d) can be worked in four groups – one running, one returning, one waiting and one moving into their starting position.
  A fun way of giving everyone a fairer chance to taste success is by means of handicap races. In these the poorer runners are given an advantage by allowing them to start nearer the finish, and thereby also producing more exciting and competitive ends to races.

Handicap Sprint (fig. R10)

2nd 3.7 1st 3.6

Timekeeper

Sprint Pressure (fig. R11)

1st 4.5

3rd 4.7

2nd 4.6

4th 4.8

HANDICAP Winner off Scratch: 2nd off 1 metre
3rd off 2 metres and 4th off 3 metres

(i) **HANDICAP SPRINT** (fig R10) for 4 to 8 runners.

Equipment: 4 marking cones, 1 stopwatch, a clipboard, pen and paper are needed.

- Race in pairs.
- Time each runner (10th second = 1 metre, or 1 metre = 10th second) and write down their times and resulting handicaps.
- Next run handicap races, in pairs, in which the faster runner starts from the proper start line ('Scratch') and the slower in their appropriate position.
- Run subsequent races with changed pairings.
- Finally run handicap races in groups of four.

(ii) **SPRINT PRESSURE** (fig R11) for 4 to 6 runners.

Equipment: 4 marking cones, 1 stopwatch, a clipboard, pen and paper are needed.

- Individuals race over 30 metres and record their times, and handicaps as for the Handicap Sprint, then . . .
- No. 1 races against no. 2. Both walk back to the start.
- No. 1 then races against no. 3, and both walk back to the start.
- Finally no. 1 races against no. 4, and both walk back to the start.

The walk back after running provides a brief recovery.

The sequence is repeated with each of the four runners racing the others in turn over successive runs; 2 starting off against 3, 3 against 4, and 4 against 1. Make a list of each runner's record of wins, losses and times.

Because young athletes are individuals, and like all children develop at differing rates, it is up to the coach to make judgements as to where he chooses to commence instruction, and the exact stages by which he/she will progress it.

RELAY RACING

THE BASIC MODEL

Relay running is a particular form of co-operation in running, (page 66). It is a team event in which all runners play their part, before passing on the task to another, and thereby enable the team to reach a pre-determined finish as quickly as possible. All members of the team participate. Relays provide an enjoyable way of getting children to run quickly.

With younger age groups in particular relay racing must be enjoyable. 'Tick', 'Tag', 'Tig', or Touch relays (they are all the same) are the most suitable for the very young. Touching the next runner, or carrying and exchanging small apparatus such as quoits, is more appropriate than the use of relay batons. Relay races around a track are not really right for children of this age either. There are other forms of relay which are more relevant, many of which will be found in the Relay section of the Having Fun with Athletics chapter.

It is impracticable for very young athletes to use check marks, carry in the correct hand, receive in the correct hand, or work in proper 20 metre long change-over-boxes.

SAFETY

In End File and Split File formats make sure there is sufficient space from walls so that incoming runners have sufficient room in which to slow down without hitting them. In End File and Centre File formats place a cone or other suitable marker some distance from the wall around which the runners can pass, in order to avoid injury.

INTRODUCTORY PROGRESSIONS using FILE formats.

1. 'Ticking', 'Tagging' 'Tigging' or Touching outgoing runners with the hand will be sufficient to begin with.
2. A quoit, or bean bag can next be used. It is carried in the right hand, and exchanged outside the right shoulder, by incoming and outgoing runners when using the END FILE, or There and Back format.
3 In the END FILE format, a second cone or marker can be placed between the back of the team and the wall so that the incoming runner can go around it, and approach the outgoing runner from behind. This simulates the proper form of relay exchange..
4. A change-over box can be drawn on the ground (length optional) and the object exchanged within it.
5. The next progression is to encourage the outgoing runner to be on the move when the exchange takes place, but it must still be made within the designated Change-over Zone.
6. After that encourage the runners to work out when to start running, so that a fast movement through the change-over zone can take place.
7. Provide markers and encourage performers to use them as Check Marks.
8. Finally measure (in foot-lengths) and record Check Mark distances for use another time.

Relay batons can be used as a progression beyond quoit or bean bag carrying from stage 2 onwards. Centre File formations are more effective than End File ones for progressions 4 to 8.

'CLOSED COURSE' RELAYS

The type of relay addressed in this section comes near to that which is normally seen in adult competition, and which is run on a near elliptical course, loosely referred to as 'circular'. The proper, adult, form involves a team of 4 runners, each of whom runs the same course distance (100 metres) before passing on the baton to a colleague. Precise details of the exchange procedure are set out in the later 4 x 100 Metre Relay section.

At all levels of competition tactical decisions need to be made concerning:
- the method of change-over to be used
- the hand in which the baton is to be carried, and thus
- the hand in which it will be received; and finally
- which runner runs each particular stage.

A point which needs be borne in mind is that relay running, unlike other sprinting events, is a team event, and that relatively slow runners can successfully participate in a team by the employment of slick baton passing.

In the early stages it really does not matter which of the two standard methods of exchange are used. More important is the fact that the method chosen is efficient, and that the runners are comfortable with it.

METHOD 1
THE UPSWEEP (see fig R12)

The outgoing runner:
- holds the palm of the receiving hand facing downwards
- making an inverted 'V' between the thumb and fingers.
- The thumb is held close to the body.

Fig. R12

The incoming runner:
- presses the baton firmly *up* into the hand.
- It is important that both hands touch during the process, or the third runner in the team will be left with no space at the end of the baton to enable him/her to pass it on.

METHOD 2 –
THE DOWNSWEEP (see fig R13)
The outgoing runner:
- holds the receiving hand high, with
- palm turned up towards the sky.

The incoming runner:

Fig. R13

- delivers the baton *down* into the receiver's palm.
There are no diminishing baton difficulties associated with this exchange.

In both methods it is the incoming runner's responsibility to ensure that contact is made, because the outgoing runner is unable to see what it taking place. Changes need to be rehearsed over and over again if reliability is to be attained.

THE 4 X 100 METRES RELAY
The exchanges take place in a 20 metre long Change Over Zone, preceded by a 10 metre long Acceleration Zone. These are marked out on the track, colour coded blue and orange on synthetic ones. The rules require that the baton is exchanged within the Change Over Zone, and the outgoing runner commences his/her run from within the Acceleration and Change Over areas.

Fig R14 indicates the best way to use the latter rule to the advantage of the very young, and young runners who will not be capable of taking full advantage of being permitted to start 10 metres before the Change Over Zone.

Exchanges must ultimately be practised at speed, as close as possible to race conditions. The baton must never lose pace through the zones. The outgoing runner must be accelerating, whilst remaining ahead, but within reach of the incoming runner.

The outgoing runner's duties are:
- to measure and place the Check Mark accurately
- to begin running at the precise moment when the incoming runner crosses it – neither before, nor after
- to accelerate as quickly as possible
- to push the receiving hand back when the call "hand" is given by the incoming runner
- to hold the hand steady - this is vital.

The incoming runner's duties are a little simpler; he/she must:
- maintain good sprinting form right through to the far end of the Change Over Zone
- get close to the outgoing runner
- maintain that position through the exchange
- call "hand" at the appropriate time
- give the baton in an unrushed but firm manner
- remain within the lane until all other teams have cleared the area.

These are a complex series of tasks for young runners to learn and then put into effect in a disciplined manner. They will be beyond the capacities of many. When and how they are introduced is an intricate interweave of many factors, and finally up to the experience and judgement of the coach. Figure R14 provides a rough guide as to what is appropriate for particular ages.

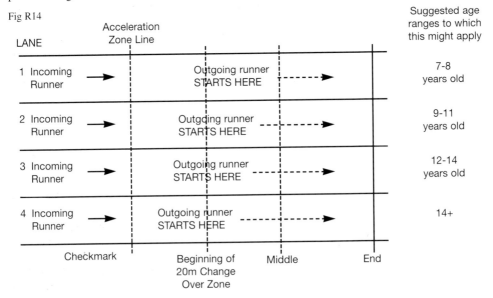

Fig R14

• Lane 1 – for *ages 7 to 8* – the outgoing runner stands with the preferred leading foot *on* the first line of the Change Over Zone, and judges when to start running; or responds to the incoming runner shouting "Go!"

• Lane 2 – for *ages 9 to 11* – the outgoing runner stands within the Acceleration Zone and uses the zone line as the Check Mark.

• Lane 3 – for *ages 12 to 14* – the outgoing runner stands on a line measured 15 to 20 feet from the Acceleration Zone line, and uses the zone line as a Check Mark.

• Lane 4 – for *14 years plus* – the outgoing runner stands at the Acceleration Zone line, on the Change Over Zone side, and a check mark is placed on the track 15 or more feet before the Acceleration Zone line.

The exact position of the Check Mark is worked out by trial and error for each runner in the Lanes 3 and 4 configurations during practice sessions. Once established, it needs to measured in foot lengths, and written down for future use.

ORGANISING AND SELECTING 4 x 100 METRE RELAY TEAMS

Because the first and third runners have to run round a bend, and thus need to keep to the inner edge of the lane in which they are running, they will arrive in the Change Over/Acceleration Zone running along its left hand side. In order to avoid collisions outgoing runners will thus have to operate on the right hand side of the of the lane. Incoming runners will have to pass from their *right* hand and outgoing runners receive in their *left* hand. This being the case the correct carrying format is:

- FIRST runner – RIGHT hand carry.
- SECOND runner – LEFT hand carry.
- THIRD runner – RIGHT hand carry.
- FOURTH runner – LEFT hand carry.

They all receive and pass the baton in the hand in which it is carried. The first runner does not have to receive, and the fourth runner does not have to pass.

It is important that all relay runners can ultimately carry, give and receive the baton with either hand, and become familiar with the requirements of running each stage of the relay, which are that:

- Runner ONE should be a good starter, and also an effective bend runner. Sometimes runners who are unreliable receivers are put in this position.
- Runner TWO should be the strongest runner, and also a good receiver and passer.
- Runner THREE should be happy and capable running a bend, as well as being a competent receiver and passer.
- Runner FOUR should be capable of maintaining form under pressure, and of receiving well.

It does not always follow that the fastest runner runs the final leg. They can often be more useful to the team in position 2, or even 1.

A useful general warm-up activity, or initial practice can involve jogging in a file while passing the baton from rear to front. Each baton carrier calls "hand" and places it into the correct receiving hand, in the proper manner. When the baton arrives at the front of the line it is placed on the ground, and picked up by the last runner in the line before the exercise is recommenced.

For older runners rehearsal of exchanges must eventually take place at speed, and over the proper distance. Working at this sort of intensity will limit the athletes to perhaps 3 to 4 runs each per session before the quality of work will diminish. This type of work provides a challenging way of working sprinters, particularly young ones.

HURDLING

THE BASIC MODEL

Hurdling is a first class running activity. It is particularly useful for young athletes because it places the running activity, and its physiological benefits, within the context of a skills challenge, and makes it more interesting and attractive to them. It should be a commonplace activity in any athletics programme for the young.

Introducing the hurdles event involves:

(a) Making it possible, and
(b) Making it enjoyable.

The initial components which need to be addressed are:

Speed   perhaps the most important of the three. It is an innate quality (fast athletes are born fast) but it is capable of being improved.

Suppleness   is the easiest to improve. Regular practice brings about a good response.

Skill   regular rehearsal, will bring improvement, but only if the correct technique is practised.

It is wrong to view hurdling as an alternative option for the less successful sprinter. Such an approach brings quite the wrong 'animals' into the event.

Criteria for success which go beyond the three initial components may include:

Height or more specifically length of leg; particularly for boys – who as adults will have to cope with 106.7cm/3'6" barriers

Frequency or natural leg speed between hurdles; particularly for girls.

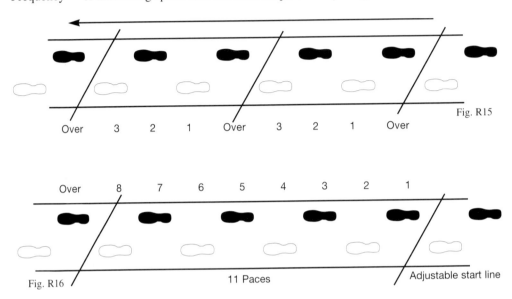

Fig. R15

Over 3 2 1 Over 3 2 1 Over

Over 8 7 6 5 4 3 2 1

Fig. R16

11 Paces

Adjustable start line

HOW TO INTRODUCE HURDLING

The first step is to establish a hurdling rhythm without neglecting the importance of running speed. To do this:

(a) Place 4 to 5 rods (sticks, canes, doweling, 22mm plumber's plastic piping) on the ground, 6 to 8 paces (3 running strides) apart. The distance needs to accommodate the age, height or ability of the group, or individuals within it (fig R15) after an approach of 11 running strides to the first rod. Runners should be encouraged to:

- run freely over these rods, stressing speed for 1, or more attempts
- step over with the SAME foot each time that a rod is met – this will produce a '1-2-3-over' rhythm
- formally clarify which foot they use to step over the rods – this is generally referred to as the 'LEAD Leg' (the other is called the 'Trailing leg').

(b) Next pay attention to the approach in which:

- each runner should place the lead foot BEHIND them at the start, or toe the start line with the foot of their trailing leg which should produce an 8 stride run to the first rod, crossing it on the 9th.

It may be necessary to move the starting position a short distance ahead of, or behind the start line in order to accomplish this for some individuals (fig R16). Very tall athletes may find the 8 stride rhythm to the first barrier difficult. They should persevere and use short fast steps at the outset, rather than reduce the number of strides to 7.

ONCE RUNNERS ARE ABLE TO SPRINT 8 STRIDES TO THE FIRST BARRIER, AND MAINTAIN A 3 STRIDE RHYTHM BETWEEN THE OTHERS THE EVENT HAS BEEN MASTERED. Subsequent development is merely a question of acquiring a more efficient technique which accommodates the barriers as they gain in height.

The Hurdles Teaching Grid (fig R17) is a useful device which enables each individual in the group to find a barrier spacing which permits them to run quickly and express themselves freely. As confidence improves they should be encouraged to move to wider spacings. It is particularly useful for such a grid to be permanently marked out at a suitable place.

Hurdles Teaching Grid

Fig R17

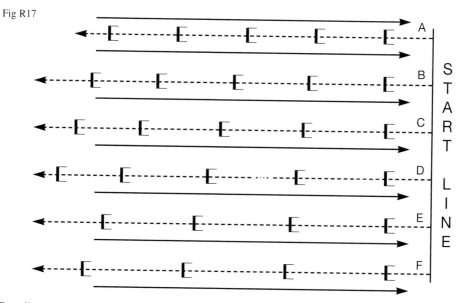

Details:
1. All runners begin from a common start line
2. All first barriers are placed 11 paces/metres beyond this.
3. Subsequent barrier spacings increase from flight A through to flight F (say at 50cms a time) although all barriers in any given lane are the same distance apart.
4. All runners commence running over flight A, and progress towards F as ability dictates.
5. They eventually find that spacing which is right for them, and work and remain there, until such time as they improve sufficiently to be able to move on to the next wider spacing.
6. All turn right at the end of the each flight to return to the start.

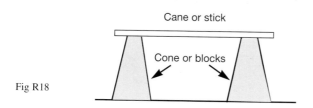

Cane or stick

Cone or blocks

Fig R18

(c) Blocks of wood, bricks, skittles or games cones can be used to increase the height of the barriers when the time comes to do so (fig R18). They can be raised 10 cm at a time up to a height of 30 cm and should enable runners to progress to working over greater heights at speed and without fear.

Fig R19

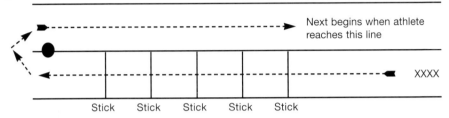

Next begins when athlete reaches this line

Stick   Stick   Stick   Stick   Stick

XXXX

Fig R20

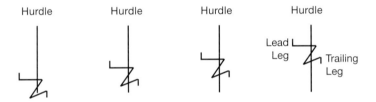

Hurdle   Hurdle   Hurdle   Hurdle

Lead Leg   Trailing Leg

UP TO THIS POINT THERE IS NO NEED TO ADDRESS HURDLING TECHNIQUE and hurdling is presented as an exciting, active speed event.

Fun competitions which encourage the 3 stride rhythm include:

• races over 5 barriers, against others in adjoining lanes, and through a common finish, and

• relay races over 4 to 5 barriers, then round a cone before sprinting back down the right hand side of the barriers (fig R19).

(d) Beyond barrier heights of 30-40cm (depending upon the average height of the runners) the teaching of the rudiments of hurdling technique becomes necessary. The key skill-drills can be established in the following way:

   (i)   Leading leg – It is, in a way, an exaggerated form of the running action. The preferred lead leg will have already been established in the preceding activities:

• Run over the appropriate line of 4 to 5 barriers using a 3 stride rhythm.

• Begin over the centre of the first barrier.

• Gradually move towards the side of the trailing leg, so that by the final two barriers only the leading leg is actually going over them (fig R20).

• Make subsequent runs entirely down the trailing leg side so that only the lead leg passes over them.

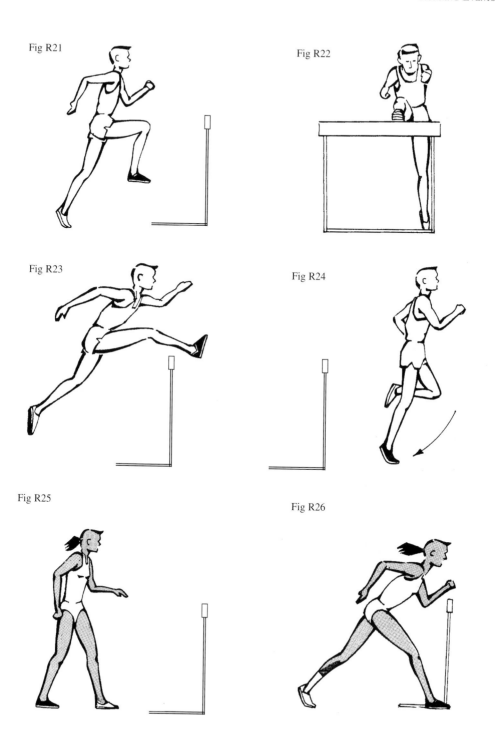

Fig R21

Fig R22

Fig R23

Fig R24

Fig R25

Fig R26

Fig R27

Fig R28

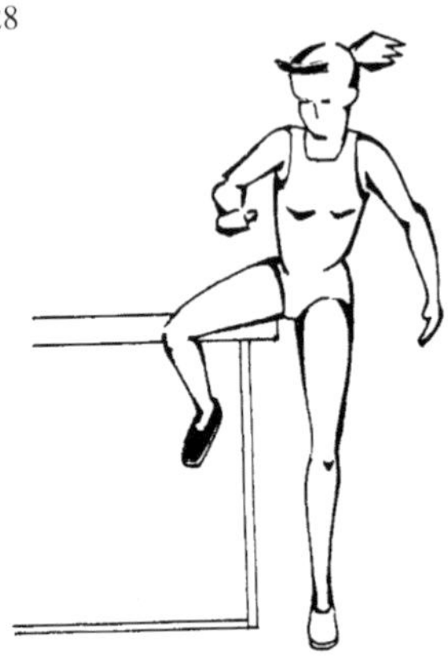

Fig R29

Fig R30

The main coaching points are:
- A fast, bent leading knee at the barrier (fig R21),
- but not too high (or the hips will sink).
- Kick straight forward at the barrier, with toe up (fig R22) – imagine a ball sitting on top of the barrier and kick it skywards.
- Hook the heel of the leading leg over the barrier – like a coat hanger onto a rail (fig R23).
- Pull it down once it is over the barrier.
- Fast down, and strike away (fig R24).
- Don't 'lock' the leading leg as it comes down.

ii) **Trailing Leg** Skill-drills become necessary above 40-50 cms. The action demands greater attention since it is less natural than that of the leading leg.

Preparation:
- Work down the leading leg side of 4-5 barriers set at half the normal spacing.

- Place the foot of the trailing leg on the ground 70-100cm away from the barrier (fig R25)
- Take a long step to place the foot of the leading leg on the ground directly in line with the barrier (fig R27).

Execution:
- Drive the knee of the trailing leg forwards with ankle tucked in and foot turned outwards (fig R26).
- Bring the knee up-and-around into the final line of running (fig R28).
- Drive the trailing leg to the ground, once it has come into the line of running (fig R29). Don't 'pose' in the recovered position.
- Run away into a strong first step off the barrier.

The main coaching points are:
- Lean forward, to establish a straight line through the hip to the ankle of the trailing leg at the presentation, as shown in fig R26.
- The arms balance the leg actions – the opposing arm swings forwards on the long step.
- Keep the knee slightly higher than the foot.
- Keep the whole action close to the body.
- Don't let the knee of the trailing leg drop too soon.
- The knee must lead the action (not the foot).
- The whole action must be fast and fluent.
- Don't let the hips sink – they stay high throughout.

DRILL FAULTS AND CORRECTIONS
Fault

Correction

a) Difficulty in placing the lead leg adjacent to the upright

Place a marker, such as T-shirt, just before the correct spot (fig R30) and have the athlete jog and step over it.

b) Leaning to the side of the leading leg in order to bring the trailing leg through.

Keep the body weight central by keeping the shoulders level.

iii) **Over the Middle** At this stage the barrier can be raised to 60cm or 70cm and all that has been learned brought together as a whole action.
Coaching points additional to those already made:
- Keeping the shoulders 'square' to the line of run
- Keeping the head still, and eyes focused ahead
- Reaching forward with arm opposing the leading leg
- Recover the same arm rapidly to the rear.

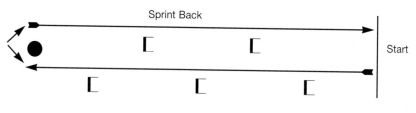

Fig. R31

TRAINING COMPETITIONS

Promote small technique competitions throughout the learning process in order to retain a speed focus. The hurdle up and sprint back activity referred to earlier is useful in this respect, and is capable of being modified in the following ways:

- Hurdling up the trailing leg side of the line, and only going over with the leading leg, and then sprinting back to the start.
- Hurdling up the leading leg side of the line, and only going over with the trailing leg, and then sprinting back to the start.
- Working alternately, using the leading leg over the first barrier, and trailing over the second, and so on to the end, before sprinting back to the start. The barriers need to be set to their respective sides as shown in fig R31.
- Out over the middle of the hurdles and sprint back to the start.
- Hurdle out, and hurdle back. A return set of hurdles is needed facing back to the start.

ACTIVITIES USEFUL FOR LATER TRANSFER TO 400 METRE HURDLING

Working the other way round, with trailing leg as leading leg, and vice versa. This can be done by drilling down the opposite sides to normal, leading with the 'wrong' leg over 4 or 5 barriers, and then trailing the 'wrong' leg. With very young athletes it is best to learn hurdling techniques leading with either leg before firm preferences have been established.

These activities will facilitate an easier transition later to 400 metre hurdling, and its need to use alternating leading legs at particular times in the race. The degree by which alternating options are pursued in technical training is a personal choice on the part of athlete and coach. If followed, the key elements of hurdling technique still apply.

200 metre and 300 metre hurdling offer excellent intermediate participatory opportunities. The event specifications are:

Event	Distance to 1st barrier	Distance between barriers	Distance to finish	Number of barriers
200 m	16 metres	19 metres	13 metres	10
300 m	50 metres	35 metres	40 metres	10

HURDLING SAFETY

a) If normal hurdles are used:
- Never cross them in the wrong direction.
- Always ensure that the barrier 'feet' are pointing towards the runner.

b) Hurdles with counterbalance weights attached can be troublesome, either
- Remove the weights, or
- Set them at the position which produces the lightest toppling resistance.

c) Avoid hurdling on wet grass.

d) If using canes, bind both ends of each cane in order to prevent the possibility of injury as the result of them splitting. Placing corks on the ends of every cane is even safer.

e) Whichever type of barrier is being used, make sure that all are in a good state of repair, and that they will collapse easily if contact is made.
- Some Local Authority Education and Recreation Departments have chosen to place a unilateral ban on the use of canes as barriers. T-shirts, skipping ropes or team braids can be laid on the floor as acceptable improvisations. When greater height is required, foam or plastic wedges (commercially available) provide an acceptable alternative.

ENDURANCE RUNNING

GENERAL CONSIDERATIONS

Track Middle Distance, Cross Country and Road Running are the main endurance activity options for the teenage runner. The distances which they run are obviously shorter than those contested by adults. The rules debar those under 11 years of age from competition. They sometimes compete in the 11 to 13 age group. Long Distance, and Marathon running is organised only for adults.

Recommended maximum *racing* distances for 11 to 15 years olds are:

	Ages 11 & 12		*Ages 13 & 14*	
Track	Boys 3000m	Girls 1500m	Boys 3000m	Girls 1mile
Road Running	Boys 5000m	Girls 3000m	Boys 6500m	Girls 3500m
Cross Country	Boys 2½ miles	Girls 3000m	Boys 3 miles	Girls 3500m

Some time ago the Medical Commission of the IAAF recommended that athletes younger than 14 should not run distances of more than 800m. This was later modified so that it referred only to racing. The advice was abandoned at a later date. The point that they were attempting to make still remains relevant.

Be wary of early specialisation. It doesn't fit with what young athletes NEED. Don't forget that they gain greater benefit from a more balanced, all round approach. It is all too easy to immerse self and athletes in the plethora of middle distance, road running and cross country events which overwhelm the winter.

THE BASIC MODEL

In speed events the coaching focus is placed on speed and technique. In endurance running it is placed on the development of endurance qualities. For older athletes this will involve a modicum of speed, speed endurance and strength endurance work in order to attain the desired performance status. Such work is wholly unsuitable for those in the younger age groups.

Some activities involve tiring the athlete to such a degree that the body is working without oxygen. This is referred to as anaerobic work. Young athletes should not be required to undertake anaerobic training. They should run aerobically - with oxygen. This implies that runs should be made at a relatively easy tempo (at a heart rate of 150 to 170 beats per minute). This is called Steady State running, A rough guide is that they should be able to converse comfortably whilst running.

It is also important that they should not train too often. The coach must thus be careful to monitor each individual in the group, since running which is aerobic for one athlete may be anaerobic for another. This can be done by taking frequent pulse counts. The athletes can be taught to do the counting themselves, placing their hand on their heart, whilst the coach times.

Strength endurance training, which includes hill and sand hill running, harness running, running wearing weighted jackets, or fast short interval running, is NOT suitable for younger athletes. Whilst these types of activities can add variety and interest to the running diet, indulgence for young athletes should be occasional rather than regular.

FORMS OF AEROBIC ACTIVITY

- Easy runs.
- Easy cross country runs.
- Easy paced interval runs, with suitable recovery (these can be done on the track, or over grass or varied terrain).
- Continuous relays, or Paarlauf relays (page 52).

- Easy orienteering competitions.
- Most games, especially major team games.

PACE JUDGEMENT RUNS
These involve working at a comfortable pace and working out:
- How fast am I running?
- How fast should I be running?
- Making speed adjustments in order to meet the target.

RUNNING CIRCUIT TRAINING - see page 40-41
- A few exercises (not too demanding) performed at temporary halts on a jogging trail.
- A routine of the same sort of exercise performed in a gym or sports hall, or at the track. Allow adequate recovery between different exercises, and don't worry too much about quality of work.

Overall pulse rates should remain between 150 and 170 beats per minute.

SPRINTING AND SPRINT DRILLS
Drills are of value to the young endurance athlete since they address the skill of running and the establishment of an efficient running action by making it:
- more economical, and
- capable of delivering effective speed surges during racing.

Such activity is generally used to link warm up to the hard graft part of the session. The work requires discipline and powers of concentration. It is thus important for the coach to explain the reasons for what is being done, and to see that it is done correctly.

CHANGE OF PACE
The ability to change pace effectively is closely linked to an efficient running technique. Fartlek running (pages 61 and 89) helps to develop this ability. The key words remain occasional, and without stress. Relevant activities are best disguised as games.

Steeplechase Relay (Indoors) for teams of 4 to 8 persons

Start

You need
3 large gymnastic mats, 3 cones, top two sections of a vaulting box, stopwatch, result card and biro

Finish

Fig R32

TACTICS

The capacity to introduce speed surges into a race, and to slow it down, is also coupled to the ability to change pace, and run efficiently. It is also linked to the athlete being in the right race position at the right time. Whilst representing adult training objectives rather than young athletes ones, the establishment of these abilities is more successful if they are addressed early in the running career. They ought to be addressed occasionally throughout the young athlete's development.

STEEPLECHASE

Steeplechase presents special problems because the obstacles are too high for youngsters, and cannot easily be lowered. It also remains the only event which, at the time of writing, has not yet been effectively opened up to female participation.

It is worthwhile for young endurance athletes to learn the skills of hurdling since it provides excellent, relevant mobility training for endurance athletes. It can also offer good balance and rhythm running experiences, in addition to laying in store useful steeplechase experience for those who may later turn to the event.

The obstacle course relays suggested in the earlier relays section of this booklet possess some features in common with Steeplechasing. Additional activities which replicate the various skills of the event can be easily devised, such as –

Special Indoor Steeplechase Relay.
- Construct a course similar to that in fig R32.
- One or two practice runs are needed, in order to become familiar with the requirements.
- The stopwatch is started when the last person crosses the start line, and
- stopped when the first runner returns.
- Race, time, and record.
- Display the best time and group number of the group achieving it on the scoreboard.

ENDURANCE SESSION IDEAS FOR 12-13 YEAR OLDS

(a) *Aerobic running*
- Easy runs or Cross Country runs, *under adult supervision.*
- Running steadily for no more than 15 to 20 minutes.
- Up to 2 times per week.

(b) *Fartlek*
- Start with an easy jogging run.
- Quicken pace for short spells, as and when the group or coach feel it appropriate – e.g. fast up short sharp hills, and recover by slow easy jogging down the slope.

(c) *Whistle-stop Fartlek*
- Work in sub-groups of 4 to 6 runners.
- Each group needs a leader, who selects the route during the run.
- They set off jogging. The coach times.
- After 2 minutes the coach blows a long blast on a whistle, when the groups change to sprinting.
- This is terminated after 10 seconds by a double whistle blast,
- The group change to walking for 20 seconds, during which the leader is changed.

- A triple whistle blast recommences a spell of 2 minutes jogging, and the whole cycle is begun again.

Each cycle can be repeated as many times as the group can sustain interest and energy.

(d) *Interval running*

Interval running involves alternate bouts of hard and easy work. The hard elements should be easy paced for younger athletes, over relatively short distances, and the recovery should be a walk back to the start. There should be 2 minutes of additional recovery between every set of 4 runs, e.g.:

- 2 sets of 4 x 60 metres, or
- 2 sets of 4 x 80 metres, or
- 2 sets of 4 x 100 metres.

The coach controls the workrate by talking to the group, and by setting target times to which the group must keep. Use of a whistle blast at the beginning and end, and even in the middle, enables the group to make pace adjustments and learn the 'feel' of running at that particular pace.

Refer to the Relays part of the Athletics Games section for ideas in which (4.1), (5.1), (5.2), (6), (6.1) and (9) are particularly appropriate.

(e) *Pace Judgement activities*

The ability to judge running pace is important to endurance athletes, and activities which promote this in practice are useful in developing this capacity.

Activity 1

Equipment   2 stopwatches, plus cones if you wish to use them to mark the course.
Target   To run 100 metres in 22 seconds, without using a stopwatch.

Rules/procedure
- Prior practice, using a stopwatch is permitted. Several attempts can be made.
- Compete in pairs to see who can get closest to the target time for running the course.
- A whistle can be blown when the time is up.
- Make several runs and score the competition like a golf tournament with runs won, halved or lost.

Activity 2

Equipment   Stopwatch, plus cones to mark start and finish, a result card and a pen or pencil.
Organisation   Group divided into teams of 3 to 6 persons, one of whom acts as leader.
Target   To run the course at a pace acceptable to the group.

Rules/procedure
- The leader carries the stopwatch (check how to use it before starting).
- The whole group runs 'On the spot' or 'In place' about 10 metres before the start.
- On the leader's command all run forward together at a speed which is comfortable for everyone – it is *not* a race.
- The leader starts the stopwatch as they pass the first cone, and stops it as they pass the second.

- The time is noted, and the group walk back to the start, discussing the run as they do so.
- If no one was discomforted then the run is repeated, attempting to do *exactly* the same time, with the leader calling out the time from the stopwatch.
- See which teams are most consistent in meeting their target times.

(f) *Lucky Spot Circuit Training,* and

(g) *Odds and Evens Circuit Training*
(See page 41) are recommended activities for young endurance athletes.

(h) *Aerobic Games*
Such as Domes and Dishes and Capture the Flag (pages 19 and 21) are suitable for most age groups although they probably appeal most to the very young.

RACE WALKING

THE BASIC PRINCIPLES
The rules state that walking is: "A progression of steps so that unbroken contact with the ground is maintained".

They then go on to clarify that at each step the advancing foot of the walker must make contact with the ground before the rear foot leaves the ground. It is this requirement which distinguishes walking from running. In all other respects walking is simply an additional endurance event.

POSTURE
- Walk tall, and
- with relaxation.
- Keep trunk erect, or with only a slight degree of forwards lean (5 degrees).
- Avoid leaning backwards.
- Focus attention at the track, 25 metres ahead - not at the feet.

TEACHING
- Technique before speed.

DEVELOPMENT
When youngsters are first introduced to walking there will be a tendency for them to mimic what they think they see in walking. They move their hips from side to side in an exaggerated manner. This, the coach should stop at the outset. Some sideways movement will eventually occur, but it will happen gradually as the result of other technical improvements. The aim is to get as much of the movement as possible going forwards.

INITIAL INTRODUCTION TO TECHNIQUE
The following drills are done over a distance of approximately 25 metres:

(1)   WALK TALL AND RELAXED, with:
- arms hanging loosely at your side
- at slightly faster than normal pace, so that some effort is being expended.
- The supporting leg must not be permitted to bend, or the walk will develop into a run.

(2)   Next, BRING THE ARMS INTO PLAY:
- bent at the elbows like a runner does.
- They move across the body, but
- not beyond the centre line of the torso, and
- not above chest height.
- The hands come back as far as the hip bone on each back swing.
- The shoulders remain low.

(3)   THE FEET should:
- touch the ground heel first, with
- toe up.
- They roll from heel to toe.
- The toes make the final push against the ground.

(4)   THE HIP ACTION should:
- happen naturally as the result of
- placing the feet on the centre line of the walk, which is learned by
- placing them so that their INNER edges touch a line marked on the ground, or
- an imaginary line on the ground.

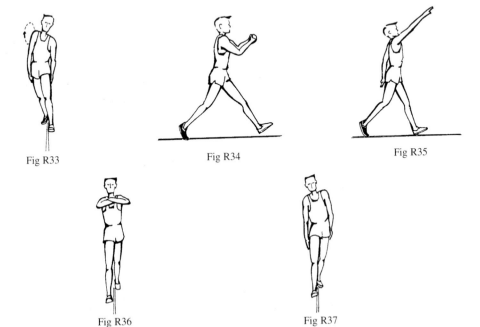

Fig R33

Fig R34

Fig R35

Fig R36

Fig R37

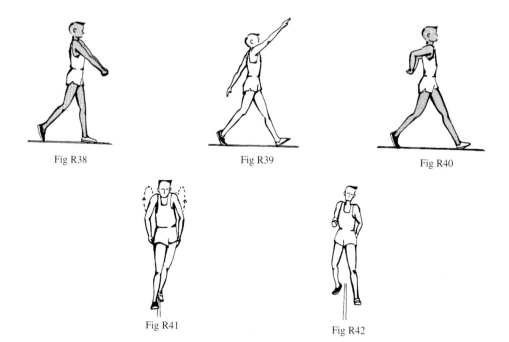

Fig R38   Fig R39   Fig R40

Fig R41   Fig R42

INTRODUCTORY DRILLS AND PRACTICES

Like most drills they can be used to forge a link between warm up and the main session. Carry out the first drill for about 40 seconds, then follow it with a minute's walking at various speeds before embarking on the second drill, and so on.

The drills are listed in the order in which they should be carried out. They should be done regularly, but slowly at first, so that the correct movements are firmly established before speed injections are made later.

Drill 1 – *Objective: Shoulder isolation*
- Walk along a straight line using strides of medium length.
- Arms hang by your sides.
- Rotate the left shoulder backwards (fig R33).
- Rotate the right shoulder backwards

Drill 2 – *Objective: To get the feeling of body movement*
- Raise bent arms (90 degrees at the elbow) to shoulder level (fig R34)
- Clasp hands.
- Walk with *long* strides.
- Placing feet on either side of a straight line drawn on the ground.
- Move arms to right and left to balance the motion of the pelvis whilst
- keeping your chest to the front.

Drill 3 – *Objective: Mobility work on shoulders.*
  • Walk along a straight line using medium strides.
  • Hold one arm straight down by your side, while
  • rotating the other backwards, fully extended (fig R35).
  • Repeat with the opposite arm.

Drill 4 – *Objective: Pelvic movement.*
  • Fold your arms in front of your body at shoulder level (fig R36).
  • Walk, placing your feet either side of a straight line, using medium strides.

Drill 5
  • Walk along a straight line using *short* strides
  • Hold both arms by your sides.
  • Lower your right shoulder as your right leg passes under your body (fig R37).
  • Do the same with your left shoulder as your left foot passes.

Drill 6 – *Objective: Rear leg drive.*
  • Walk along a straight line using *short* strides.
  • Clasp your hands low down in front of your pelvis (fig R38)
  • Balance the rotation of your pelvis as you walk by moving your hands from side to side, whilst
  • keeping your arms straight.

Drill 7 – *Objective: Co-ordination of arms and leg actions.*
  • Walk along a straight line using *short* strides.
  • Circle extended arms backwards(fig R39) whilst
  • keeping in time with walking steps.

Drill 8 – *Objective: To feel the pelvic movement.*
  • Walk placing your feet to either side of a straight line, using medium strides, while
  • clasping both hands behind your back, at hip level (fig R40).

Drill 9 – *Objective: To improve rhythm and relaxation.*
  • Walk along a straight line using *short* strides .
  • Keep your arms down by your sides, whilst you
  • circle both shoulders backwards (fig R41).
  • Co-ordinate the shoulder circling with your walking strides.

Drill 10 – *Objective: Pelvic mobility.*
  • Walk along a straight line using strides of medium length, but
  • place your feet a considerable distance to either side (fig R42).

FURTHER ACTIVITIES TO DEVELOP SOUND TECHNIQUE

Posture

25 metre Shuttle relays carrying bean-bags on the head. They may not be touched until within the final metre before change over, and during change over itself.

Leg action

(a)   Walk quickly with arms stretched sideways, and hands *above* shoulder level. This activity indicates whether legs and hips are working correctly.

(b)   Later, individuals start with arms outstretched, but on a signal bring them into normal use.

(c)   Walkers slalom between a row of 6 to 8 cones placed 1 to 2 metres apart.

(d)   Athletes stride between battens, or canes placed on the ground 30 cm apart.

(e)   Participants walk alongside one another, about 3 metres apart, passing a ball.

(f)   Individuals walk around a track dribbling a football; keeping the feet low and just moving the ball forwards on each contact.

JUMPING EVENTS
THE PRINCIPLES of TEACHING THE APPROACH

GENERAL

Beginners should commence their approach run from a standing start. They should 'toe' the start mark with their take-off foot, because this is the easiest concept to both understand and remember. The other foot should be placed to the rear. The resulting approach run will be composed of an even number of strides (2,4,6,8,etc.) as appropriate to the time and stage of learning, fig J1.

Short approaches are slower and safer than long ones. They are therefore more appropriate for the initial stages of learning, and particularly to younger children. They should be lengthened only as the ability of the performer or group dictates that it is safe to do so. It will be necessary to upgrade the quality of landing facilities; from gym mats to sand pits, and foam beds, as this occurs.

Except in the High Jump the following are useful rule of thumb guides as to the eventual competitive lengths which approaches should reach for average performers:

- 10 running strides for 10 year olds
- 12 running strides for 12 year olds
- 14 running strides for 14 year olds.

This approximates to one running stride for each year of the child's age. High Jump approach runs need to be shorter - 6 to 8 running strides.

Fig J1

Fig J2

RUNNING STYLE DURING THE APPROACH
This should emphasise:
- running 'tall', or with high hips (fig J2)
- running on the balls of the feet
- running lightly, and
- maintaining an upright body position, especially during the final stages into take-off.

THE BASIC TAKE OFF MODEL
The basic take off is a *high* hop, made with, or without a late in-flight change of leg. The hop has a *'one to the same'* structure. The 'leg change' turns it into a *'one to the other'* 'jump, see page 100. The key instructional points are that:

- The hips go UP. — Tie a braid or handkerchief to a post placed just ahead of the take-off, as a target.
  Get the jumpers to try to raise their hips to it.

- There is THRUST through the take-off leg — It 'pushes the ground away', or the skin is stretched behind the knee of the jumping leg as it takes up an extended position in early flight.

- The free thigh is PUNCHED HIGH — Moving away from the take-off leg.
- It is held there, AT HIP HEIGHT.
- The torso maintains an ERECT position.
- The arms EXAGGERATE THEIR RUNNING ACTION. — In High Jump, and in the Step and Jump take-offs of the Triple Jump they synchronise in a simultaneous forward swing.

- If a free-leg change is made, it takes place right at the end of flight.

The basic High Jump is a scissors jump, and may be either a derivative of a high hop, or a high 'leg-change', or Scissors.

The basic Long Jump is a derivative of either a high hop, or a high 'leg-change', which finally becomes a 'one to two' jump.

Basic Triple Jump involves a 'one to the same' jump, followed by a 'one to the other' jump, and is rounded off by a 'one to two' jump.

The basic Pole Vault take-off is a high hop.

Figures J3 and J4 show the two basic models for jumping take-offs.

Fig J3   Fig J4

THE BASIC FLIGHT MODEL

Safety factors dictate that at this level High Jumping is a Scissor Jumping activity, and fits neatly into the following flight model covering all jumping events:
- Head UP, and
- Body ERECT, fig J5.

The High Jump scissor action is a bent legged affair, not straight legged.

In Pole Vault at this level there is minimal flight, yet the general flight model still fits. Encourage vaulters to keep their hips and shoulders facing forwards while swinging on the pole. Discourage them from turning towards it.

Fig J5

BASIC LANDING MODELS

Landings in Long Jump, Pole Vault and the final phase of the Triple Jump are made on two feet. They should be 'squashy', and absorb the force of landing by bending at the ankle, knee and hip joints, fig J6.

The single footed landings of the hop and step phases of the Triple Jump are described as being 'active' or 'clawing', in order to illustrate the fact that the foot should meet the ground travelling backwards, so that the jumper is driven forwards, fig J7. This contact with the ground should be essentially flat footed.

In the Scissor form of High Jump the landing takes place with the body in an upright position. The free leg makes the first ground contact, quickly followed by the take-off leg.

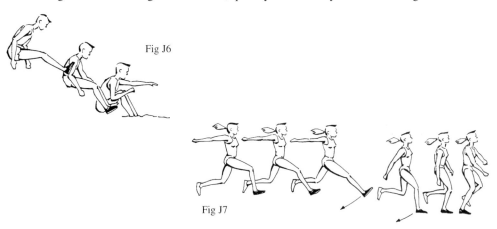

Fig J6

Fig J7

PREPARATORY JUMPING ACTIVITIES

Physical Educationalists recognise FIVE basic forms of jump. These are:
- from ONE foot to the SAME foot
- from ONE foot to the OTHER foot
- from ONE foot to TWO feet

- from TWO feet to TWO feet, and
- from TWO feet to ONE foot.

The first of these is a hop, the second a leap (or step), the third a 'sail' jump, and the fourth our familiar standing Long Jump.

The final two forms have no athletic relevance at all, except that the 2 to 2 structure is used in many of our award schemes and test batteries and that is why it is familiar. From the technical standpoint it has no part to play at all, since it doesn't conform sufficiently closely to the technical requirements of any jumping events for really effective transfer of technical training to take place.

WHAT TO TEACH

Primary Physical Education seeks to provide opportunities for children to explore jumping activities and to become competent in a wide range of jumping skills. The work can be presented either as a teacher/coach directed activity, or as a series of child centred tasks. Additional to the basic forms of jumping listed above many aspects of flight and landing will be explored. Throughout the educational approach the key words used will be "what happens if . . . ?" or "can you . . . ?". The same approach is highly appropriate in clubs for children of similar ages.

TYPICAL TASKS MAY INCLUDE:
1. Make a standing '2 to 2' jump.
2. Make a standing '2 to 2' jump for distance.

3. Make a standing '1 to 2' jump.
4. Make a standing '1 to 2' jump for distance.

5. Make a standing '1 to 2' jump over a low obstacle.

6. Make a standing '1 to the OTHER' leap.
7. Make a standing '1 to the OTHER' leap for distance.

8. Make a standing leap over a low obstacle.
9. Make a standing leap over a low obstacle, and run on.

10. Walk a few steps to make a '1 to 2' jump for distance.
11. Walk a few steps to leap for distance.

12. Walk a few steps to make a jump onto a raised landing area, such as the top section of a vaulting box, or a high jump landing module.
13. Walk a few steps to make a leap onto a raised landing area.

14. Walk 4 steps and jump for distance.
15. Walk 4 steps and leap for distance.

16. Walk 4 steps and jump onto a raised landing area.
17. Walk 4 steps and leap onto a raised landing area.

18. Run a few steps and jump for distance.
19. Run a few steps and leap for distance.
20. Run a few steps and jump onto a raised landing area.
21. Run a few steps and leap onto a raised landing area.

22. Run 4 steps and jump for distance.
23 Run 4 steps and leap for distance.
24. Run 4 steps and jump onto a raised landing area.
25. Run 4 steps and leap onto a raised landing area.

26. Make a standing '1 to the SAME' hop.
27. Make a standing '1 to the SAME' hop for distance.
28. Walk a few steps and hop for distance.
29. Walk a few steps and hop onto a raised landing area.

30. Walk 4 steps and hop for distance.
31. Walk 4 steps and hop onto a raised landing area.

*32. Run a few steps and hop for distance.
33. Run a few steps and hop onto a raised landing area.
*34. Run 4 steps and hop for distance.
35. Run 4 steps and hop onto a raised landing area.

36. Make a standing 2 hops and a jump.
37. Make a standing 4 hops and a jump.
38. Make a standing hop, leap, and jump (Triple Jump).
39. Make a standing 2 hops, leap and jump.
40. Make a standing 2 hops, 2 leaps and a jump.
41. Make a standing 2 hops, 2 leaps, and 2 jumps (this activity has great kinaesthetic feel).

42. Run a few steps into a hop, leap, and a jump (Triple Jump).
43. Run a few steps into 2 hops, leap (step) and a jump.
44. Run a few steps into 2 hops, 2 leaps (steps) and a jump.
45. Run a few steps into 2 hops, 2 leaps (steps) and 2 jumps.

46. Run 4 steps into a Triple Jump.
47. Run 4 steps into 2 hops, step and a jump.
48. Run 4 steps into 2 hops, 2 steps and a jump.
49. Run 4 steps into 2 hops, 2 steps and 2 jumps.

50. Walk into a hop, to head a suspended target such as a football.
51. Walk into a hop, to raise your hips level with a target tied to a post.

52. Run a few steps, to head a suspended target such as a football.
53. Run a few steps, to raise your hips level with a target tied to a post.

54. Run 4 steps, to head a suspended target such as a football.
55. Run 4 steps, to raise your hips level with a target tied to a post.

56. Run a few steps to leap over a cane, rope or bar.
57. Run 4 steps to leap over a cane, rope or bar.

N.B. – Activities prefaced with an asterisk are getting towards the edge of the safety limits which permit landings onto hard surfaces, even if covered by gymnastic landing mats. They are safest if made into sand pits.

HIGH JUMP

SAFETY
This event should carry a government health warning, especially where young performers are concerned.

Fosbury Flop is dangerous. It could damage your health – permanently.

Because of this it presents a teaching/coaching dilemma. To what extent does one accede to the exciting images of the event portrayed by television and introduce Fosbury Flop, or does one sublimate the thrill of mimicking the champions, as well as the good kinaesthetic feel which the event envokes, and hold to *safe*, sound teaching and technical practice by teaching the Scissors style of jump? One dare not abet enthusiasm and motivation, however appealing, at the expense of safety.

Our inability to guarantee safe foam landing facilities at every venue where young high jumpers may be required to jump, even though they may be available at the teaching/training venue, points us unequivocally in one direction – that of the Scissor jump.

Fosbury is a great jumping experience, but it is too dangerous to be taught to children.

THE APPROACH
The fact that it should commence from a standing start in which the take-off foot 'toes' the start mark, and that it should be between 6 and 8 running strides long has already been established. So has the fact that short approaches are safer than long ones. These precepts govern how we start to build the High Jump approach run.

Begin with a 4 stride approach, and lengthen only as improving ability dictates. Since jumping safety requires that the take-off should be made close to the base of the nearer bar support stand, the approach run must become so grooved that it brings the jumper consistently to that spot.

Adjustments may need to be made to the starting position to either shorten or lengthen each run until the correct length for each particular jumper has been established. This will be indicated by the position in which the take-off foot has landed at the end of each run. Those jumpers who take off from their right foot must approach from the left hand side of the landing area as they face it. Those who take off from their left foot must approach from the right hand side, fig J8.

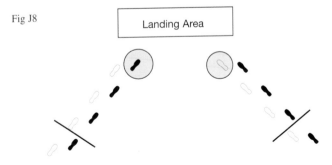

Fig J8

Landing Area

THE TAKE OFF

High jumpers should be discouraged from taking off until their approach run is secure and consistent.

The take off should take place close to the base of the nearer bar support stand. Draw a 50cm diameter circle on the ground at the correct spot and encourage beginning jumpers to abort attempts which do not bring them into that circle. Each individual take off should hold to the basic principles for take off listed on page 98. At take off the jumper's torso should be erect, and their 'tail' tucked in, under their spine (fig J9).

Fig J9

Fig J10

FLIGHT

The basic technical model for the Scissor action is a bent leg one (i.e. the free leg is *not* kept straight, but is bent at the knee joint). The concept of making the jump encased in a glass cylinder, without breaking it, is a helpful one, fig J10. The torso should remain firmly fixed in an upright position, with the tail tucked in. A *late* 'leg-change' occurs in flight.

PREPARATORY ACTIVITIES

1. Activities 3, 5, 12, 13, 16, 17, 20, 21, 24, 25, 26, 29, 31, 50, 51, 52, 53, 54, 55, 56, and 58 of those listed on pages 100-101.

THE BEGINNINGS OF PROPER HIGH JUMP

2. Draw a 50cm diameter circle on the ground at the base of each bar support stand.
3. Take 4 large paces from the centre of each circle at an angle of 30° to the bar.
4. Mark the spot where each fourth step lands. This will be the start of the approach run.
5. Get the jumpers to arrange themselves in a line, at their correct start mark, according to the foot from which they make their take off.
6. Get each jumper to 'toe' the start mark with their take-off foot, when their turn to jump comes round.
7. Get them to run one – two – three and *jump,* making a gentle Scissor jump onto the landing area.
8. They must walk back to the end of each working group after jumping.

This routine establishes the basic format for the Scissor jump. Individual adjustments to the starting position will be necessary. It will need to be brought closer to the take-off position if they are failing to reach the take-off circle, or further away from it if they are running beyond the correct take-off spot. Only when this is secure and consistent is it safe to progress any further.

9.   Introduce a low elastic bar, fig J11.
     Elastic bars are available commercially, or can be easily made from a 4.5m length of 1″ wide elastic. The elastic tends to pull the bar supports inwards. Be sure to **arrange the base so that the longest part of it points towards the centre of the bar, and to weight it down.**

10. Raise the bar progressively as improving ability dictates.

Fig J11

THE FINAL ACT

The first session will probably terminate at stage 8 or 9. The approach run, so carefully established, will need to be measured in order to be able to set it out for subsequent sessions. The measurement is best made in the following way:

• in foot lengths
• making the measurements as shown in fig J12.

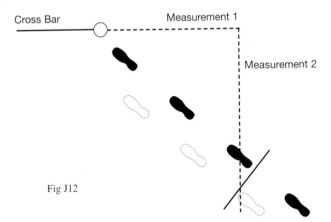

Fig J12

LATER DEVELOPMENT

The approach can be lengthened, by two running strides at a time, either by:

• the coach/teacher taking 2 large paces, or
• each athlete measuring 10-12 further foot lengths along the line of approach.

   It is possible to change the approach to a curve, ready for later use in Fosbury Flop, by using the template set out in fig J13.

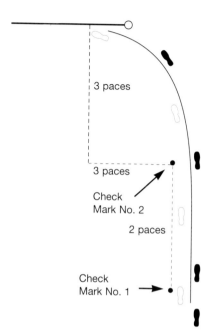

3 paces

3 paces

Check
Mark No. 2

2 paces

Check
Mark No. 1

Fig J13

Most jumpers ought to be able to run this approach in 6 strides. Timid ones may take 8 strides. Those using 5 or 7 will need to make changes to their starting position, provided that they are not 'toeing' the start line with the wrong foot. The 7 stride version of the approach run will need shortening by one running stride. The accuracy checks set out after step 7 above will need repeating until the run is consistent and secure.

Finally, light the blue touch paper and let them Scissors jump from a curved approach. This format requires three measurements to be taken in order to be able to reconstruct it accurately on another occasion. They are shown in fig J14.

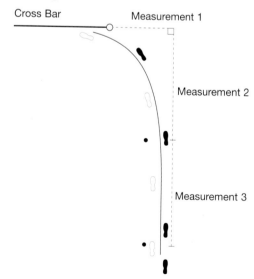

Cross Bar   Measurement 1

Measurement 2

Measurement 3

Fig J14

LONG JUMP

THE BASIC TECHNICAL MODEL

The basic technical model is a 'Stride' jump, fig J15. In this the thigh of the leading leg is kept ahead, and away from that of the take-off leg, for as long as possible during flight. The torso is again held erect. The take-off leg is only brought to its landing position alongside the free leg at the last possible moment. The action is most effective if the leg is brought through folded, as a short lever, rather than swung from the hip as a long one.

At take off the jumper should concentrate upon:
- remaining high
- getting lift
- punching the free leg to hip height in front of the body , and
- working the arms vigorously (that opposing the free leg upwards, and the other backwards) as in fig J16.

Fig J15

Fig J16

SAFETY

Sand pits are not essential for jumps made from a standing start, or from a very short approach of 4 strides. This type of jump can be safely made onto floor or ground. Accumulative long term safety is best served by using gym landing mats to land on, and doing the event as an occasional activity. Gymnastic 'crash' mats of the type used for tumbling activities can be useful when working from longer approaches, with older performers. Special care must be taken to make sure that they do not slide forwards when used indoors. Sand pits become important when approach runs get longer, and landing forces increase as a result. It is very important that these are dug before use, rather than just raked, and are kept clear of buried debris.

TEACHING

The early teaching model is a 'one to the other' jump, or leap, fig J17. Start with standing jumps, in which the main focus should be upon:
- use of a powerful leg thrust. and
- use of a simultaneous arm swing.

Maintain the focus by making the following demands as the work is being done:
- Measure ordinary jumps without use of thrust or arm swing
- then thrust back against the ground, or swing the arms as the jump is made.
- Measure it.
- Compare this with the previous effort.

Most performers should have jumped further as a result of the exercise. Elicit what has been learned about jumping far.

Fig J17

PROGRESSING FURTHER

(a) Standing 'one to the other' jumps are useful for developing awareness of the need to keep the free, or leading leg, and take-off thighs apart in flight.
(b) Standing jumps, made from a height of 30-50cms, are useful for illustrating the relevance of height in jumping far.

Generally the distance travelled from a height will be in excess of that attained from ground level, and will serve to reinforce the instructional point.

Instructional points

These are relevant at all stages of development.
- The take-off leg should thrust hard against the ground.
- The torso should remain upright in flight.

- The head should look up in flight.
- The thighs should stay apart in flight.

The very young need to be given opportunities to repeat these activities many times, over several years, in order to absorb the skills and gain the relevant basic experiences which will then carry forward securely into later work.

TAKING IT FURTHER

If work to determine the preferred jumping leg has not yet been covered then time must be spent on it before proceeding further. This can be done by getting the jumpers to move about freely and make occasional *high*, relaxed one to the same, or one to the other jumps. Have them jump first from one foot, and then the other. After several attempts on each they should be able to decide which they prefer to jump from. Once a clear decision has been arrived at they should stick to jumping from that foot.

When completed, follow the listed developmental stages:

(1) Select a take-off area so that performers are not troubled by the need to be accurate at this stage. Such may be either the space between the take-off board and the pit, or a specially made large plywood take-off board, say 30 x 50cms. The latter can be safely fastened to the ground alongside the jumping pit, as shown in fig J18, by using 6" nails pushed through holes drilled around the corners and edges.

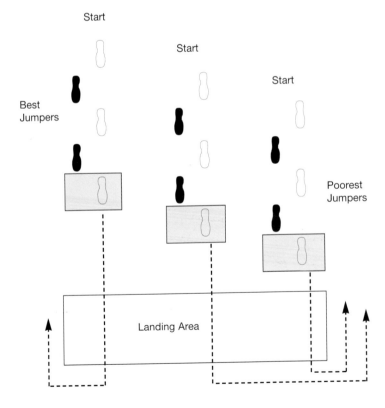

Fig J18

108

(2) Pace back 4 large paces from the centre of the take-off area, and place a start mark on the ground.

(3) Get the jumpers to stand with their preferred take-off foot at that mark when beginning their run.

(4) They then run and jump. Most will take 4 running strides. A small number will take 6. A few may take 5 strides and take off from their wrong foot as a result. Move these people a little nearer the landing area. Put a special mark down for them if necessary, although they should be able to judge this special starting position relatively easily in relation to the main group starting mark.

A very small number may run 5 strides yet take off from their correct foot. These people will have inadvertently begun with the wrong foot at the start mark. Check that they have their correct foot at the mark each time that they begin their run. Remind them each time that they jump if necessary.

(5) Further minor adjustments to run length will be necessary in order to tailor each run to the individual. These can be made during several jumps. Jumpers will need to remember their particular start in relation to the group mark.

(6) As the final act at the end of this session jumpers will need to MEASURE THE LENGTH OF THEIR OWN RUN IN FOOT LENGTHS and note it for future use. This can be done in individual record books , or in a class/group book kept by teacher/coach.

(7) The first act in all subsequent Long Jump sessions is to measure out that distance and mark the beginning of each personal approach run.

. . . AND FURTHER

(8) Set a target to which the jumpers attempt to raise their hips when jumping, fig J19. This can be done by tying a braid or handkerchief to a post set just beyond take off. It should be at a height roughly level with the jumper's shoulders.

Fig J19

(9) Work from a slightly raised take-off area in order to provide more time in the air, and to give the sensation of jumping high. Old gymnastic beat boards, spring boards or a strong specially made take off box (fig J20) will do the trick. Two or three gym benches placed side by side will also suffice *provided that constant care is taken to make sure that they remain close together during use.*

Fig J20

TRIPLE JUMP

Triple jump is a technically uncomplicated event in which physical capacity and conditioning play a large part in success. It is stressful to bone structures, especially growing ones, and ought therefore to be no more than an occasional activity for young athletes.

FUNDAMENTALS

The basic technical model is a hop, immediately followed by a step (or leap), and immediately finished off by a jump. Each element blends smoothly into the next. Landings are made on the same foot as the initial take-off, then on the other foot, and finally on both feet, fig J21. Ground contact should be essentially flat footed, with the foot moving backwards.

High, large hops detract from the overall success of the jump, because horizontal speed, critical to the successful execution of the subsequent two phases, is lost. For all jumpers the step phase is the weakest and requires most attention. The front thigh should be kept at hip level and the landing should be delayed as long as possible. It is important to keep the torso erect through all phases of the jump. Simultaneous use of the arms is a feature of the step and jump take-offs for good quality performers.

Fig J21

Hop   Step   Jump

EARLY INTRODUCTION

The very young should be exposed to a broad diet of multiple jumping experiences involving combinations of hopping, leaping and jumping like those described on pages 100-101. They can be dressed up as 'hop scotch' tasks. The original format is shown in fig J22.

Fig J23 shows a form which demands a succession of hops terminated by a jump

Fig J24 shows a form demanding a series of steps, or leaps terminating in a jump.

Fig J25 involves a mixture of hops, leaps and jumps (2 of each).

Fig J26 shows how the task can be adjusted so that it makes quality demands, each element requiring more effort than that preceding.

Fig J22

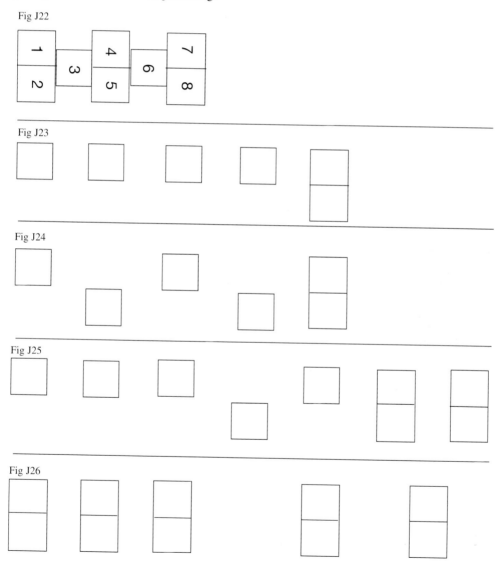

Fig J23

Fig J24

Fig J25

Fig J26

SKILL INTRODUCTION
This is quite simple. Demonstrate, then get the participants to work alongside you and copy, as follows:
1. Stand with the preferred foot forward,
2. make a tiny hop onto that foot, then
3. step onto the other foot, and finally
4. jump onto two feet.
5. Pause briefly after each landing.

Instructional points:
- 'Drop' onto each landing.
- Make each landing on flat feet.
- Keep each element bouncy.

Some very young athletes may experience difficulty in hopping, or linking the hop to the step. They can be given additional hopping practice, or encouraged to hold their non-hopping leg behind them (fig J27) during the early part of the hop, releasing it just before the landing and step are made.

Fig J27

DEVELOPMENT
Once the basic format of the event has been established then increased effort can be encouraged; firstly through larger hops, steps and jumps, and then by the expedient of adding:
- a walk-on approach
- a jog approach, and finally
- a running approach.

Grids like those shown in figs J28 and J29 are very useful in this respect. The lines are drawn to prescribed relationships between the phases, so that they demand the correct values of hop, step and jump whatever the overall distance jumped. They thus help the jumper to apportion effort correctly.

Jumpers begin where the lines are drawn closest together but then work towards wider spacings through successive efforts until they find their optimum jumping position, i.e. that in which they can jump as far as possible yet land on each line in turn. Generally increased effort will be needed, particularly through the step phase of the jump, and performers will need to be encouraged to thrust hard out of the hop landing, and to hold their free thigh high during the flight phase of the step.

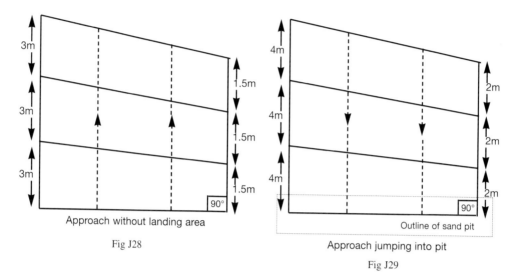

Fig J28 — Approach without landing area

Fig J29 — Approach jumping into pit

Indoor work in which the sequence terminates in a jump onto the top sections of a vaulting box, or onto a set of wallbars, is useful in setting the focus upon jumping up during the first phase.

SAFETY and ORGANISATION

From standing starts and short approach runs landing into sand is not essential, unless accurate measurement is sought, although it is possible to measure jumps made onto floors, or playgrounds if the under part of the heels are chalked before the jump is made. As the approach lengthens sand pits into which to finish the jump become more necessary.

POLE VAULT

Pole Vault is generally an activity for older children – those over 13 – but useful preparatory experience can be given to those of younger years. This involves confidence building activities such as balancing on a pole, and swinging on it. Proper poles are not essential. Five or six foot long wooden, bamboo, or metal staves are quite adequate, provided that they are light enough to handle comfortably, and strong enough to bear the weight of the user in that particular activity. If in doubt test them out yourself. Lengths of PVC plumbers' waste piping have been successfully used for young, light children.

ACTIVITIES PROVIDING PREPARATORY EXPERIENCES:

GENERAL ACTIVITIES
(1) All hanging and swinging activities that are possible on climbing frames, and ladders.
(2) From gymnastics – backward rolls, cartwheels and round-offs.
(3) Inverted support, and inverted hanging, fig J30.

Fig J30

MORE SPECIFIC ACTIVITIES

(4) "How high can you climb?" See fig J31.

The pole is held vertically by each user, with one end on the ground, and they see how far they can climb before it overbalances and they come down. The pole(s) can be taped or painted at regular intervals in order to assist measuring and assessment.

Instructional point:
- Make sure that the feet are freed in order to land safely.

Fig J31

(5) "How long can you stay on the pole?" This is similar to the previous activity. The vaulters climb to a prearranged point and stay there as long as possible. They can be individually timed using a stop watch, or when groups are involved to a count in second intervals called out by leader, teacher or coach.

(6) Stab and swing, fig J32. The pole is held in front of the body, with *right* hand, and both thumbs, uppermost above head height. Left handed vaulters should have their *left* hand uppermost. They walk and plant the distant end of the pole on the ground ahead of them, and swing themselves past it gripping firmly as they do so. The landing is made on two feet. This activity can also be performed as a 'one to the same' activity, in which the free leg remains off the ground throughout the swing and landing.

Fig J32

7) Vaulting the stream, fig J33. A make believe stream is marked on the ground using chalk, or by laying down skipping ropes. The task is to place the distant end of the pole into the stream, and vault safely from bank to bank.

Instructional point:
- Land with feet, hips and shoulders facing forwards.

Fig J33

115

8) Vaulting the widening stream.

This activity is the same as Vaulting the Stream except that the stream is constructed so that it gets wider at one end. The vaulters start at the narrow end. Having vaulted safely from bank to bank, without going into the stream, they move one step towards the wider end on their next attempt. The challenge is to see how far each can get without getting 'wet', and which gets nearest the wider end of the stream.

(9) Riding down, fig J34.

This takes place from a height, standing on a gym box, table or steeplechase barrier, into a sand pit, or onto a gym 'crash' mat.

Instructional points:
- The pole is held vertically, and close to the box, table or barrier
- the *right* handed vaulter stands with *left* foot forward, and
- grasps the pole in front at shoulder height, with
- *right* hand uppermost, and
- both thumbs uppermost.

Left handed vaulters reverse the instructions in italics.
The vaulter pushes off and swings past the pole to land on two feet.

Instructional points:
- Hips and shoulders must remain facing the front, and
- a tight hold must be kept on the pole until the landing has been made.

Fig J34

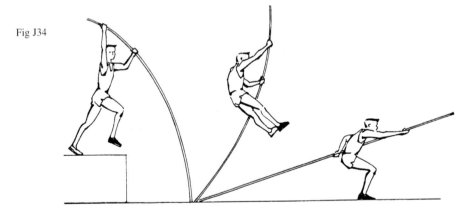

ADDITIONAL ACTIVITIES

(10) Backward roll, fig J30.

(11) Rope swing onto a vaulting box, or table, fig J35.

(12) Backward roll to clear a cane supported six inches off the ground.
- The progression in this activity is to raise the cane stage by stage.

(13) Stab and swing to a wall, fig J36.
- The stab is made close to a wall; the vaulter swings to place both feet on the wall on either side of the pole and then returns onto the feet on the ground as the pole swings back.

Fig J35

MORE ADVANCED ACTIVITIES

(14) Riding down to clear an elastic bar on the way.
  • This activity is very similar to number 9. but a low elastic bar is placed between take off and landing and has to be cleared on the way down.
  • Raise the height of the bar as the vaulters gain confidence.
  • The instructional points of activity must still apply.
(15) Stab and swing over an elastic bar into a sand pit, fig J37
  • This is a combination of activities 6 and 14. It begins with a short approach run of 4 or 6 strides.
  • Pace out a general start mark taking 4 or 6 large strides back from the take-off spot, in a similar manner as for Long Jump or Triple Jump.
  • The distant end of the pole is stabbed into the nearer end of the sand pit.
Instructional points:
  • The landing is made on two feet, with hips and shoulders facing forwards.
  • The grip on the pole is retained until the landing has been completed.

Fig J36

Fig J37

EVENT SPECIFIC GAMES

LONG OR TRIPLE JUMP CHALLENGE

Game objective	To jump your farthest individually, and as a team.
Rules	• Measure from toes on take off, to heels on landing. • Sitting back after landing *may*, or *may not* be permitted, as you decide. • The PAIR with the greatest total of their best jumps wins, or • the PAIR with the greatest total of ALL jumps wins.
Equipment	Measuring tape(s), clip board, result sheet and pencil.
Organisation	Players work in pairs. One jumps whilst their partner checks and marks. Measure. Change places and repeat.

LONG JUMP TEAM EVENT

Game objective	To cover the course in as few jumps as possible.
Rules	• It may be either a partner or team competition. • Pairs or teams jump in rotation. • The first jump is made from the start, and subsequent jumps from the marker. • The marker is picked up by each jumper before each jump, carried with them during the jump, and placed level with their heels after landing. • The PAIR or TEAM covering the course in fewest jumps wins.
Equipment	Course markers, Jump markers (one per pair/team).
Organisation	Mark out the course long enough to take several jumps to complete. Organise pairings or teams.
Progression	(a) Series of 2 to 2 jumps. (b) Series of 1 to 2 jumps. (c) A mixture of the above.

TRIPLE JUMP TEAM EVENT

Game objective	To cover the course in as few TRIPLE jumps as possible.
Rules	• It may be either a partner or team competition. • Pairs or teams jump in rotation. • The first jump is made from the start, and subsequent jumps from the marker. • The marker is picked up by each jumper before each jump, carried with them during the jump, and placed level with their heels after landing.
Equipment	• The PAIR or TEAM covering the course in fewest TRIPLE jumps wins.
Organisation	Course markers, Jump markers (one per pair/team). Mark out the course long enough to take several jumps to complete. Organise pairings or teams.

STAB & SWING CHALLENGE

Game objective	To Stab & Swing your farthest individually, and as a team.
Rules	• Measure from toes on take off, to heels on landing. • Sitting back after landing *may*, or *may not* be permitted, as you decide. • TWO hands must be kept on the pole throughout each effort. • The PAIR with the greatest total of their best jumps wins, or • the PAIR with the greatest total of ALL jumps wins.
Equipment	Vaulting, ash or bamboo pole(s), measuring tape(s), clip board, result sheet and pencil.
Organisation	Players work in pairs. One jumps whilst their partner checks and marks. Measure. Change places and repeat.

STAB & SWING CHALLENGE

Game objective	To cover the course in as few Stab & Swings as possible.
Rules	• It may be either a partner or team competition. • Pairs or teams Stab & Swing in rotation. • The first Stab & Swing is made from the start, and subsequent ones from the marker. • The marker is picked up by the partner of team member before each jump, and placed level with the vaulter's heels after landing.
Equipment	• The PAIR or TEAM covering the course in fewest Stab & Swings wins.
Organisation	One vaulting, ash or bamboo pole per team, course markers, jump markers (one per pair/team). Mark out the course long enough to take several Stab & Swings to complete. Organise pairings or teams.
Safety	Special care needs to be taken if long poles have to be used. Teams must work with sufficient space between them so that they are not put in danger by the pole of nearby teams.

THROWING EVENTS

THE PRINCIPLES OF COACHING THROWS

Despite their prominence in the athletics programme, the throwing events in the United Kingdom are generally not well taught – they are often not taught at all. Perhaps the cause is fear – fear of the safety implications, or fear arising out of lack of knowledge on the part of coach or teacher. Both are poorly founded. Safety is really just a matter of common sense, and no person exists who is unable to express him/herself by throwing since it is a basic human activity. Indeed only those who have suffered the grave misfortune of having both arms amputated are completely incapable of the act. We all have some knowledge, and this starting point, at some stage is the same for everyone – even the Olympic champion.

MAKE THE EVENT FIT THE ATHLETE
The rule book will decree that a boy in the under 15 age group must compete with a 4kg shot. A 3.25 kg shot is specified for girls of the same age. Some competitors in this age group will have only just passed their 13th birthday. There is a large discrepancy in size and strength. Some girls at this age will be larger and stronger than some boys.

It is thus very important that the size and weight of implements supplied for teaching and practice are such that the user can perform the event skill comfortably. A range of implements of different weights should be on offer so that everyone coming for coaching can work at performance levels which are right for them. In order to be fair to other competitors in the event the rule book *fits athletes to the event*. In teaching and coaching terms this is a recipe for failure.

SOME RULES HAVE TO BE BROKEN
In establishing the early skills of throwing events it is best to disregard several other competition rules. Throwing circles, stop boards and other restraining lines inhibit freedom of movement. They should be discarded, until the bases of the event technique have been firmly established. Then, and only then should the performer be placed within the constraints imposed by the rules of competition.

IMPROVISATION
A lack of light, or specialist equipment should not deter us from introducing throwing events. Suitable improvisations involving javelins made from canes or doweling; discoi from plastic hoops, rubber quoits or cut from softwood; hammers from quoits and rope or footballs enclosed in sacks; and shot from stones or blasting shot encased in old socks are very much the order of the day. Details of how to construct then are given in the Coaching Young Athletes – Coaching Theory Manual companion to this booklet.

PRACTICE MAKES PERFECT
There is a high correlation between the number of throws taken and attainment. The opportunity to make numerous throws, in a safe environment is paramount to successful learning.

Dispense with tape measures. It is not necessary for the performer to know the exact measurement of every effort, and measuring uses up valuable practice time. Useful feedback can be obtained just from the flight path of the implement. Special markers, which are moved when implements are recovered, can be used to indicate best individual efforts, or if preferred lines drawn on the ground at selected intervals.

FEW THROWS = few successes.

'DRY' DEMONSTRATION

No, it's not a cocktail; it refers to posing in selected positions, with or without the implement, in order to demonstrate certain aspects of skill. If you can't throw, don't – just pose. Alternatively, you can go through the pattern of the movement slowly. Demonstration is a useful way of teaching a skill since 'a picture is worth a thousand words'. 80 per cent of what we learn comes from what we see. Children between the ages of 8 and 13 are particularly good mimics of movement.

THE BASICS

Refined aspects of technique only count for 5 per cent of performance. The basic essentials of the throwing events, those things which are taught to the novice, contribute 95 per cent to the distance thrown. These basics are easily acquired, and are well within the scope of the non-specialist coach. THE RULE IS – keep it simple.

COMPETITION IS THE SPICE OF LIFE

Following the initial satisfaction gained from throwing things through the air, the coach will have to provide further motivation in order to maintain interest. This can be delivered through *competition*. Measurement will be necessary if one session's activity is to be carried forward to the next. It is possible to get to a measuring stage in the developmental process by the end of the first session. This done each youngster involved will be able to come away from the experience with a personal best performance. Noted down, such a performance can be used as the motivation for the next session, and success in bettering it for that to follow.

Competition can be organised in several ways – target competitions, team competitions, handicap competitions and most improved, but that which is most important is competition against oneself for that lasts throughout life.

SAFETY FIRST

Throwing is an inherently safe pastime which can prove deadly. Danger only lurks when mistakes are made. It is the duty of the coach to ensure that the thrower is placed in a safe environment, created by common-sense principles, such as:

- "all throw – then all retrieve"
- "look before you leap, *or throw*"
- "check all equipment".

These precepts, and others which will be revealed later in the text, form an essential part of throwing discipline and care for others. Provided that time is taken to instil such control and awareness throwing is a safe, stimulating and satisfying activity.

THIS TEXT

Throwers belong to either of two main categories: the majority are right-handed, whilst a very small remainder are left-handed. Rather than write the text entirely for right-handed throwers,leaving those who are left-handed to transpose it, the option to refer to the 'preferred', or 'throwing', hand or side (right for the right-handed, or left for the left-handed) has been taken, where appropriate.

THE BASIC THROWING MODEL

The four throwing events look dissimilar to the casual observer. Some are rotational, one employs an approach run, whilst another is two-handed. Although three take place from circles, one of these is larger than the others. A more discerning eye will detect similarities between all four events which link them together and can be looked upon as *Common Root Movements*, or:

- WEIGHT TRANSFER – from right to left (for the right handed thrower), or from start to finish. The final delivery is initiated by the rear leg, which rotates as it drives the hips around and forwards, and transferring body-weight to the left(front) leg as it does so (fig T1 all sequences a) to d)).
- LEGS FIRST, ARM(S) LAST – so that the strong, but slower moving leg muscles provide the initial acceleration (fig T1 all sequences (a) to (c)), whilst the weaker, but fast moving muscles of the arms are most effective adding force to an implement which already possesses momentum (fig T1 all sequences (d)). The arms are thus brought into play **last and fast.**
- EXTENSION – involves the thrower starting low, and finishing high so that the implement is released from an extended, high position.
- LEFT/RIGHT SIDE BRACE – means that the left side of the right-handed thrower should resist, or brace against the final rotation of the body around its vertical and transverse axes, so that the right side accelerates around it. Beginners generally fail to do this and collapse the left side and shoulder diminishing the amount of force that they can apply to the implement. A strong, high, braced release position (fig T1 all sequences (d)) should be taught.

Fig T1

SHOT

DISCUS

JAVELIN

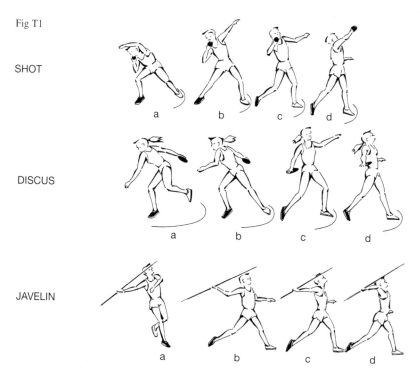

a   b   c   d

- TORQUE – is created by keeping the hip axis ahead of the shoulder axis (fig T1 all sequences (c)).This creates a spring-like action which, when released, adds an explosive movement to the final action.
- ROTATION – is essential to all throwing events. Where it is not an integral part of the technique, as in hammer, discus and rotational shot put it is explicit through the final delivery actions, and very young children should have these experiences as part of preparation for later involvement.

These experiences can be gained from work involving the throwing of bean bags, quoits, hoops, small balls, shuttlecocks, soccer or netballs and medicine balls. Throwing can be fun, and should be made fun. This is done safely by not being restricted to standard implements and special devices like foam and sponge javelins, discoi, shot and hammers have been specially developed in order to aid this type of work.

PREPARATORY THROWING ACTIVITIES

It is important that children aged 7 and over should be introduced to the basics of throwing. At this stage it is not necessary to turn them all into Olympic performers. It is more important to give them enjoyment, and a small modicum of achievement from slinging, flinging, pushing and heaving objects a long way. Children in the 7 to 11 age group should be exposed to as great a variety of throwing experiences as possible, particularly of the types depicted in Figs T2 to T16.

LARGE BALL BASICS

ORGANISATION

Work the group in pairs facing each other, throwing towards each other and spaced by the distance thrown. *This is a special arrangement appropriate only for these particular early practices in which soft apparatus is used.* There are two starting positions:

(a) STRADDLE in which the feet are shoulder width apart, as if toeing a line.

(b) IN LINE in which the feet are arranged one behind the other, with *left* forwards for the right-handed, and *right* foot forwards for the left handed.

METHOD
Work through the following series of activities using questions and instructions as indicated;
In the text which follows **IP** indicates an instructional point needing to be made at that particular stage.
1. A *seated* two handed throw from the chest (figT2) – feet are in front of the thrower in a straddle position. **IP** – encourage EVEN pressure through both arms.
2. A *kneeling* two-handed throw from the chest (fig T3) – thrower kneels in the straddle position without sitting on the heels. **IP** – encourage EVEN pressure through both arms, and ask "why does the ball travel further?"
3. A *standing* two-handed throw from the chest (fig T4) – straddle stance, and even pressure. **IP** – ask again "why does the ball go further?"

Fig T2

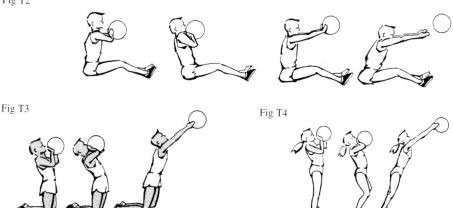

Fig T3   Fig T4

4. Repeat stage 3 – saying "see how far you can both get apart" and still encouraging even pressure. **IP** – ask "what has happened to the path travelled by the ball"? It should have gone up. The follow-up question is "what does this show us about throwing the ball a long way?"

5. A *moving* two-handed chest throw – "drive your partner backwards, keeping the same space between you; then let him or her drive you backwards" **IP** – ask "are your feet still in the straddle position?" Follow up with "what position are they in?" They should be in line.

6. Return to a *standing* two-handed chest throw, but with feet *in line* (fig T5) – *left* foot forwards for the right-handed, and *right* foot forwards for the left-handed. **IP** – "This is the correct starting position for ALL throwing from now on".

7. Repeat 6, starting with the chest turned to the *right* for right-handed throwers (fig T6) – the ball continues to be held at chest level. The thrower turns both chest and hips to the front before making the throw. Even pressure must be applied down BOTH arms.

8. Repeat 7, but remove the *non-dominant* hand just before release. **IP** – encourage rear leg and hip drive.

9. A *standing, two-handed underhand throw* (fig T7) – made from a straddle stance. **IP** – "Stretch upwards after release", and ask "which part of your body did most work"? The correct answer is – legs.

10. Repeat 9 making the hips rise – **IP** – "feel full body upwards extension".

Fig T5   Fig T6

Fig T7

Fig T8

11. A *standing* backwards, underhand, overhead throw (fig T8) – made from a straddle stance. **IP** – "Still make the hips rise, and feel extension" Ask – "what happens if you release too soon?" Follow up by asking – " what happens if you release too late?"
N.B. HOOPS, QUOITS AND BEAN BAGS CAN ALSO BE THROWN IN SITTING AND KNEELING POSITIONS.

12. A *standing* backwards, underhand, throw over the LEFT shoulder (fig T9) – straddle stance, and cup both hands *under* the ball. **IP** – "Start outside your RIGHT knee", and "finish with your chest facing your partner".

Fig T9

13. A *standing* backwards, underhand, throw over the RIGHT shoulder – straddle stance, starting outside the LEFT knee and finishing with your chest facing your partner. **IP** – "Decide which shoulder you prefer to throw over".

14. "Do a *jump turn* around the foot on your *throwing* side to make a backwards, underhand over-the-shoulder throw," (fig T10). **IP** – "Make sure that your feet arrive back in the straddle position after turning".

Fig T10

Fig T11

15. "Do a *jump turn* around the foot on the *non-throwing* side and make a backwards, underhand over-the-shoulder throw," – making sure that the feet arrive back in a straddle position after turning.
16 "Do a *half* turn round the foot on your *non- throwing* side, and take your *non-throwing* hand away just before you *sling* the ball (fig T11) – **IP** – "Land in a straddle position with your non-throwing side nearer where the ball lands".
17. Repeat 16 using a plastic hoop instead of a ball (fig T12) – the hoop should be held in one hand using an overgrasp. *SAFETY requires that, here, throwers have more space around them.* **NB –** Do not spend too much time on this activity, it teaches bad release habits, but gives good general action awareness.

Fig T12

18. Repeat 16 using a quoit instead of a hoop – **IP –** "Hold the quoit in an overgrasp so that finger tips lip the rim, just like a proper discus" (fig T13).
19. A *standing* overhead throw in a *'soccer throw-in'* style – from a straddle stance.
20. A *moving* overhead throw in a *'soccer throw-in'* style – partners drive each other backwards as in activity 5, which will again force an IN LINE working stance. **IP** – Reinforce the instructional points made in activity 5.

Fig T13

Fig T14

21. A *standing* overhead throw in a *'soccer throw-in'* style with one leg forward (fig T14) – **IP** – "*Left*, foot forwards for the right-handed, and *right* foot forwards for the left-handed."
22. Repeat 20 with *preferred* leg leading all of the time – this will force a 'shuffle' step. **IP** – "Keep moving *away* from the overhead ball".
23. "*Run* 3 strides and make an overhead throw in a *'soccer throw-in'* style" (fig T15) – **IP** – "Still keep moving away from the overhead ball". "Which foot must be forwards at the start in order to finish with your *preferred* foot forwards?"

Fig T15

24. A *standing* *'soccer throw-in style'* throw made from the SCHWANBECK position (fig T16) – the ball is withdrawn laterally and both elbows pressed outwards to make a 'window' through which the head and chest are thrust in beginning the throw. **IP** – "The chest must face the front before the arms are brought into play"

Fig T16

25. A *moving Schwanbeck-style* throw following a shuffle approach in which the *preferred* leg leads.
26. A *moving Schwanbeck-style* throw following a 3 stride running approach.
27. A *standing* tennis ball throw at a small target (coin) placed on the ground between partners – **IP** – The palm of the throwing hand must face upwards and the elbow must pass close to the ear as the throw is made.
28. A *moving* tennis ball throw at a a small target (coin) placed on the ground between partners – **IP** – "Use a shuffle step with *preferred* foot leading", and "Keep the palm facing upwards".
29. A *standing* tennis ball rebound throw – made in the same way as in 27 but close to a wall so that the ball rebounds from ground, to wall, and back to the thrower – **IP** – The ball needs to pitch within 1m of the wall.
30. A *standing* tennis ball throw at a wall target – one formed by concentric circles needs to be drawn onto a wall before use – **IP** – All of the IPs of tennis ball throwing.

SHOT PUT

THE BASIC TECHNICAL MODEL

The basis of the event is the STANDING THROW. This accounts for 90 per cent of the distance thrown.

1. The INITIAL STANCE (fig T17a) must ensure that the legs are able to be the prime movers. The aim should be to adopt what is referred to as the '*chin-knee-toe*' position in which the chin, the rear knee, and the rear toe are in vertical alignment. The feet should be either in line, or the toe of the leading foot offset so that it is in line with the heel of the rear one.
2. In the POWER POSITION (fig T17c) the rear leg should begin the movement, driving the hips round to the front, and transferring body-weight from the rear leg to the leading leg.
3. In the DELIVERY POSITION (fig T17f) the body should be tall, and extended with the leading side *braced*. It is only when the chest is facing the landing area that the arm punches the shot out. The elbow of the throwing arm must stay high.

KEY POINTS:

- Chin - knee - toe.
- Feet offset
- Hip drive
- Low to High
- Leading side brace
- Arm last and fast
- High throwing elbow.

Fig T17

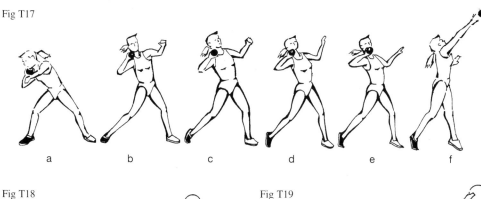

a   b   c   d   e   f

Fig T18   Fig T19

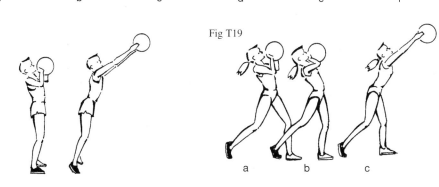

a   b   c

PREPARATORY ACTIVITIES

EQUIPMENT
Soccer balls and or 1 - 3kg medicine balls, sufficient for at least one between two.

ORGANISATION
Work in open space, such as the centre of the track, or a games pitch. Start off working in pairs.

PROGRESSIONS
1. PUSH from the CHEST
   Face your partner and make a two handed chest push (fig T18):
   - first without bending the legs, then
   - bending the legs.
   This will show how important the legs are.
2. "Change to a medicine ball, and adopt an in-line stance with the *preferred foot* ahead of the other (fig T19)." "Start with your weight on the rear foot, and transfer body-weight onto the leading foot as the two handed throw is made."
3. "Holding the ball in the *dominant* hand, but balanced by the other, adopt the 'Initial Stance' posture (figs T17a and T20a). Drive the hip on the *preferred* side to the front, and 'punch' the ball away (fig T20c).
4. Encourage competition using either of the kneeling formats indicated in figs T21 and T22. N.B. At all times ensure that the throwing elbow is kept high, and behind the ball.

Fig T20

Fig T21

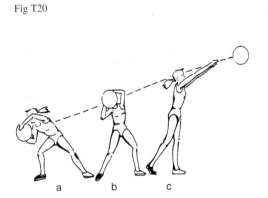

a   b   c

TEACHING PROGRESSIONS

EQUIPMENT
An assortment of shot ranging from 2.72kg to 5kg is needed. Ideally each participant should have a shot, although one between two is acceptable.

ORGANISATION
Ignore the circle. Simply use a line such as the track kerb, or a games pitch boundary, from which to throw. Arrange the throwers in pairs so that each pair is 3m from their neighbours. All throw, on the coach's command – then ALL retrieve together on the coach's command.

Fig T22

Fig T23

PROGRESSIONS

Stage One
1.   THE GRIP – is important because unless the correct grip is used distance will be sacrificed, or injury and loss of confidence ensue.
      Place the shot at the base of the first three fingers (fig T23) with the thumb and little finger providing support at the side. The first three fingers should be evenly spread (but not stretched) behind the implement. The shot should then be placed under the chin, with the elbow held high.

Stage Two
2.   STANDING FRONTAL PUT – arrange the throwers in a line, facing the direction of throw, with feet shoulder width apart. Push the shot out using arm only, ensuring that the elbow is kept high. The implement remains tucked into the chin at the beginning of the movement (fig T23).
3.   STANDING FRONTAL PUT with TORSO TWIST – encourage the throwers to twist their upper body to the rear before throwing, in order to increase range and thus put greater force into the throw (fig T24).
4.   STANDING FRONTAL PUT USING THE LEGS – encourage the throwers to bend their legs as they twist to the rear so that they can be brought into the action. This should substantially increase the distance thrown (fig T25).
      N.B. It is important that the elbow of the throwing arm, stays high, and the thumb down, during each throw.

Fig T24

Fig T25

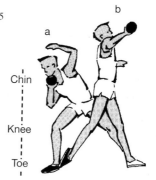

Stage Three

5. CHIN-KNEE-TOE PUT – throwers adopt the chin-knee-toe starting position (fig 25a) with feet and hips facing the *side*, whilst the shoulders are 'cocked' to the *rear*.
    The width of the stance will be between 60-90cms, depending upon the height of each thrower. Take care to see that the toes of the *rear* foot are in line with the heel of the *leading* foot (fig T17b). The throw is made by the rear leg twisting and driving its hip to the front.
    Each thrower should concentrate upon:
    - a fast hip action
    - keeping the throwing elbow high, behind the shot, and
    - following the shot right out with a fast arm extension (fig 25b).
    N.B. The *leading* shoulder should finish high whilst that side *resists*, or *braces* against the throwing action (fig 25b).
    "Think . . . body LOW to HIGH and arm LAST and FAST".

6. COMPETITION – should be encouraged as soon as a reasonable degree of competence has been established in the 'Chin-knee-toe' standing throw.

Fig T26

Stage Four

7. THE 'SHIFT' – comes next. It adds initial momentum to the throw, and produces longer throws.
    For beginners it should consist of a simple *side-on shuffle* made in the direction of the throw (fig T26). The leading leg moves one step, the rear leg closes to it, and the leading leg takes a futher step into the 'chin-knee-toe', standing throw, position.
    IP - "Shuffle low, then lift with the legs".

COMPETITION IDEAS
(a) Seated shot put – a single handed version of fig T2.
(b) Two-handed put forwards (fig T4)
(c) Measure a standing throw, then see who can add most distance using the shuffle shift.
(d) Target throw (fig T27)

Fig T27

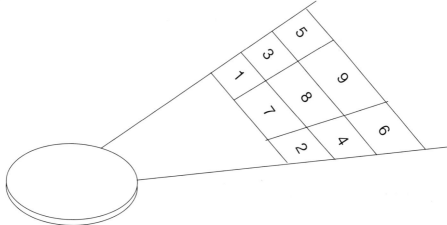

DISCUS

THE BASIC TECHNICAL MODEL

The STANDING THROW provides the basis of the event although it doesn't have quite the same importance as in Shot Put. It contributes about 75 per cent of overall distance.

1. The INITIAL STANCE utilises a similar 'chin-knee-toe' position to Shot Put (fig T28a). The discus is swung to an extended position at shoulder height, preliminary to the throw.
2. In the POWER POSITION (fig T28b) the rear leg drives its own hip round to the front in exactly the same manner as in Shot Put
3. The leading side braces against the rotation in the DELIVERY POSITION, as the thrower finishes high (fig T28d).
4. The THROWING ARM is whipped through only when the legs have completed their work, and the torso is facing the direction of throw (fig T28c).

KEY POINTS:

- Chin - knee - toe
- Feet offset
- Hip drive
- Leading side brace
- Arm last and fast

Fig T28

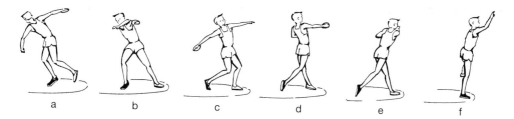

a   b   c   d   e   f

135

PREPARATORY ACTIVITIES

EQUIPMENT
Plastic hoops, and quoits are needed, sufficient for one per thrower, if possible.

ORGANISATION
Work in open space either at the centre of the track, along the kerb of the straight or along a games pitch boundary line. Begin working in pairs.

PROGRESSIONS
1. HOOP SLINGING – in pairs, slinging from one to the other using a sideways action (fig T29).
    The hoop is held in an overgrasp. A game of hoop-la in which the thrower tries to get the hoop either over the head, or the outstretched arm of their partner, can add interest and improve the fun element. The hoops are safe, except when neighbouring throwers get too close. Make sure that pairs are well spaced out.
2. HOOP SLING FOR DISTANCE – start in a conventional 'chin-knee-toe' standing throw position (fig T30).
    IP – "Use a 'long' throwing arm. Keep shoulders level. Twist hips and chest to the front". The air resistance of the hoop will ensure that the arm is used last.
3. Change to QUOIT SLINGING – using the same overgrasp hold as for hoop slinging. Place targets such as games grid cones at a conservative distance for each thrower in order to to ensure a correct movement sequence.
    IP – "Lift the quoit out using your legs. Keep shoulders level".
4. DISCUS GRIP SLING – (fig T31) in which the hand is placed so that it covers the quoit and only the end joints of the fingers support it. Because the throwing action is a palm down one, the quoit has to be supported by the non-throwing hand in the starting position.
N.B. Both hoops and quoits can be thrown competitively, and distances measured and recorded.

TEACHING PROGRESSIONS

EQUIPMENT
An assortment of discoi ranging in weight from 0.75kg to 1.5kg is needed. Young beginners need more of the lighter implements, lighter than those of their competition specification. Ideally each participant ought to have a discus, although one between two is acceptable.

Fig T29

Fig T30

Fig T31

ORGANISATION

Ignore the circle. Again use a line such as the track kerb, or a games pitch boundary to throw from but safety demands more space between adjacent throwers than for shot put teaching because of the tangential nature of a mistimed release. An echelon arrangement as depicted in figure T57 is theoretically safer. All throw, on the coach's command – then ALL retrieve together on the coach's command.

PROGRESSIONS

Stage One

1. THE HOLD – The non-throwing hand is used to support the discus by its shoulder like a golf tee supporting a golf ball.

   Fig T32

   The throwing hand is placed on top of the discus with fingers evenly spread, but not stretched, and the end joints curling over the rim (fig T32). It is important ***not*** to grip the discus but rather to let it just rest in the hand. For children who find this difficult a compromise by which it is held on the second joint of the fingers rather than the end joint is acceptable.

Stage Two

2. LATERAL SWING DRILL – performed standing facing the landing area, with feet in a straddle stance.

   The discus is supported on an extended non-throwing arm, with the throwing hand cupped over the top of it, as in stage 1. The discus is then swung away from the supporting hand into an extended position on the throwing hand side of the body, and then returned to the supporting hand. This is repeated until the thrower has confidence in the action.

   IP – Make sure that the palm of the hand holding the discus remains facing the ground throughout.

Stage Three

3. LATERAL SLING – made from the same stance as 2, but the discus is released forwards, spinning off the first two fingers (fig T33) and cutting through the air parallel to the ground. Right-handed throwers will make the discus rotate clockwise, and left-handers will spin it anticlockwise.

Stage Four

Fig T33

Fig T34

a   b   c

4. STEP BACK SLING – in which the foot on the throwing side is taken back, with the throwing arm, into the familiar 'chin-knee-toe' position. The rear leg should drive its hip forwards at the start of the slinging action (fig T34).

Stage Five
5. STANDING THROW – from an initial stance (fig T34a) in which:
- the rear leg takes up the 'chin-knee-toe' position
- the feet are placed 60-90cms apart, and
- the toes of the rear foot are in line with the heel of the leading foot.

The discus is supported in the *non-throwing* hand, and gripped as already described. It is withdrawn at speed, to an extended position behind the shoulder of the *throwing* arm. Unless this is done at speed the discus will not stay in the hand. The throw is started by a vigorous rear hip drive. The throwing arm must stay extended as it takes up the movement initiated by the hips. At this stage the thrower should be encouraged to keep both feet on the ground throughout the throw.

Stage Six
6. CORRECT FLIGHT – is important. Emphasis should be placed upon the fact that the implement should leave the front of the hand, from the first finger, moving in the direction of the thumb. This will cause it to spin in the direction indicated in 3 above. It should also cut through the air like an aircraft wing.

Stage Seven
7. Standing throw competition is appropriate at this stage.
   IP – Stress the speed of the twisting hip action as the throw is made.

Stage Eight
RUNNING ROTATION – can be next introduced. It will increase the distance thrown.
8. (a) The thrower starts at the back of the circle, or approximately 2.5m away from the throw line, in a side-stance, with the non-throwing side nearer the landing area, and feet shoulder width apart (fig 35a), and performs the preliminary swing movement.
   (b) After the back swing, the thrower takes the rear foot forwards around the other, turning

Fig T35

about the vertical axis as he/she does so, and then moves the other foot into its standing throw position. It is important that the thrower travels towards the direction of throw as the turn is made. The movement is really a simple stepping one, made along a straight line and which can be drawn on the ground if this helps.

(c) This stepping action should bring the thrower into the 'chin-knee-toe' standing throw position, after which an active *throwing* hip initiates the final sling.

Care needs to be taken when large numbers are involved and it is best for one person to throw at a time, stepping forward well ahead of the group to make their throw (fig T36) and then retiring so that the next can take their turn.

Fig T36

Throwing line

5m

x = each thrower   3m

COMPETITION IDEAS

(a) Throw plastic hoops or quoits for both distance and accuracy (fig T27).

(b) Target throwing – place a marker at a distance that all can reach – first to hit the cone is the winner.

(c) The longest throw, including the roll after landing, encourages the correct angles of release.

JAVELIN

THE BASIC TECHNICAL MODEL

The STANDING THROW is less important than in shot put or discus; nevertheless it
    contributes about 66 per cent of the ultimate distance.

1. In the DELIVERY POSITION a similar 'chin-knee-toe' position to that of the other two
    throws applies (fig T36a) in which the thrower's weight acts through the rear leg.
2. The feet should be placed in line with the line of delivery.
3. The throwing arm should be extended to the rear at shoulder level, but relaxed and with the
    hand high and palm uppermost (fig T36b)
4. The rear leg drives its hip to the front, transferring body weight onto the front foot (fig
    T36c) as it does so.
5. The throwing arm comes into the action late but fast (fig T36d).
6. The elbow of the throwing arm stays high, and close to the head, as the javelin or throwing
    ball passes almost over the top of the head (fig T36e).

KEY POINTS:
- Firm grip
- Throwing arm athletically straight
- Chin-knee-toe
- Hip drive
- Elbow close to head and javelin.

Fig T36

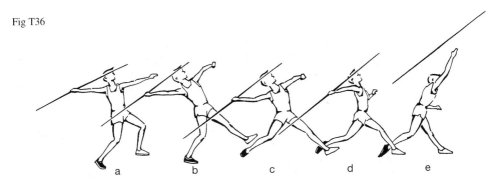

a   b   c   d   e

PREPARATORY ACTIVITIES

EQUIPMENT
Footballs and cricket or hockey balls are needed – preferably one per person.

ORGANISATION
Open space is necessary; either at the centre of the track, along the kerb of the straight or along
a games pitch boundary line. Begin working in pairs.

PROGRESSIONS
1. Start throwing a football forwards, overhead from one to the other.

Fig T37

Fig T38

Fig T39

Last two strides

- Progress to a 'Soccer throw-in' type of throw, made in the straddle position (fig T37)
  - then to a modification of it in which the arms are stretched above the head, and the 'pull' is made from well behind the body.
2. Change to an 'in-line' starting position with the *left* foot forward if right handed (fig T38). **IP** – Stress the importance of starting with the legs driving body weight onwards. The arms, as always, come into play last and fast.
3. Throw from a 3 stride approach run, in which the ball is carried over the head (fig T39). **IP** – Make sure that both feet are down before the arms are brought into play.
4. Increase the length of the approach run to five strides.
5. Change the football for a cricket or hockey ball, so that the throw is made one-handed (fig T40). **IP** – Ensure that the ball continues to be carried, and thrown, over the head, and that the elbow remains high and close to the head.

Fig T40

TEACHING PROGRESSIONS

EQUIPMENT
An assortment of javelins weighing from 400gms to 700gms should be available. Ideally each thrower should have one, although one between two is an acceptable compromise.

ORGANISATION
When teaching a group, ignore the javelin runway and work from either the track kerb on the straight, or from the boundary line of a games pitch. This permits a number of throwers to throw in the same direction simultaneously. All throw, on the coach's command – then ALL retrieve together on the coach's command.

PROGRESSIONS
Stage One
1. THE GRIP – It is important that a strong, stable grip is used. It must remain firmly behind the ledge made by the cord binding. The shaft of the javelin runs down the *length* of the palm, and not across it. The thumb and fingers, which rest against the lip of the cord grip, must press firmly on the implement in order to produce a natural spin at release.

   The three main grips (fig T41) from which to choose are:
   - (a) thumb and first finger,
   - (b) thumb and second finger, and
   - (c) first and second finger.

   In the latter it is the end joints of the fingers which rest against the binding, not the first joints.

   In Britain grip (c) is preferred for the initial teaching of the event because it encourages the palm to support the javelin, and the throwing elbow to be safely aligned. At a later stage throwers transfer to one of the others because they produce better javelin rotation about the long axis, more stability, and thus longer flight.

Fig T41

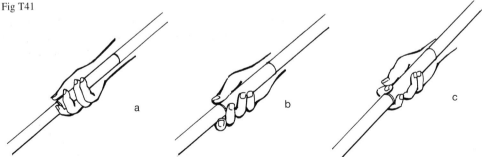

a   b   c

Stage Two
2. FRONTAL STAB – Start in a straddle stance, facing the direction of throw, with feet shoulder width apart. The javelin is held above the head, gripped firmly and pointing at a shallow angle towards the ground. The javelin is thrown/pushed into the ground about 3m ahead of the thrower. If the grip has remained firm the javelin will stick into the ground.

Stage Three
3. IN LINE THROW – Place the *leading* leg about 50cms ahead of the other, and start the throw with body weight over the rear one. Drive hard with the rear leg as the throw is made, still aiming to stick the javelin into the ground about 3m away.

Stage Four
4. THE STANDING THROW – This is the proper standing throw, as opposed to the two improper versions so far used. The javelin is launched upwards, at a shallow angle, and no longer down into the ground.

Fig T42

The javelin is held at arms length to the rear, but without the arm being rigidly straight – because this can cause a straight arm sling when the throw is made. The hand should be above the level of the shoulder, and the javelin almost parallel to the arm. The feet should be 60-90cms apart and point straight ahead (fig T42). It is important that the throwing elbow remains close to the javelin during the throwing action.

Stage Five
5. THE THREE STRIDE THROW – should be introduced once the standing throw has been mastered. It should be kept as simple as possible. The throw should continue to be made upwards at a shallow angle.

Start with feet together, facing in the direction of throw, with javelin fully withdrawn and close to the arm. The first running step is made with the *leading* foot, followed by a longer higher stride with the other. The throw is made *on* the next stride, viz:

LEFT – – – – – – BIG STRIDE – – – – – – – THROW

The big stride will bring the body weight over the rear leg, creating the standard 'chin-knee-toe' position (fig T43d) from which all throwing deliveries are made. The run should be made on flat feet, *not* on the toes. Once again the driving and twisting action of the throwing hip should be stressed.

Fig T43

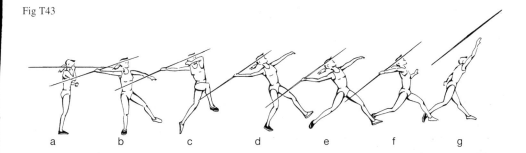

a   b   c   d   e   f   g

Stage Six

6.   LONGER APPROACH RUNS – When the three stride throw has been learned the run can be lengthened to one of FIVE strides by adding two more.
     When the five stride approach has been assimilated the approach can again be lengthened. Few beginners will get much beyond five stride throwing, but the approaches of good quality throwers are longer than this. A longer run can be built by adding two strides at a time.

COMPETITION IDEAS

(a)   Target throw at a marker cone.
(b)   Target throw into a pre-marked grid (fig T27).
   Target throwing is good for javelin throwers since it encourages throwing 'through the point', i.e. applying force along the shaft of the implement rather than across it.

HAMMER

THE BASIC TECHNICAL MODEL

Hammer is different from the other three throwing events in that:

•   the STANDING THROW contributes only a tiny percentage of the total distance thrown
•   the basic throwing stance is a straddle stance
•   the initial movements all take place with the thrower facing away from the direction of throw

Fig T44

SWINGS
These have the same function as the glide or shift in shot put and discus. They are used to impart initial speed to the implement.

The hammer is swung round the head. The arms straighten as it passes in front of the thrower, and bend as it passes behind the body (fig T44). The low point of the path followed by the hammer should be in front of the thrower's feet (fig T44j), and the high point behind the head (fig T44c). Two to three swings are usual (fig T44a-j).

TURNS
The turns are the beginning of the delivery part of the throw, and may total two, three or four complete rotations (see Fig T49). The throwers arms remain extended throughout these movements. The *preferred* foot (*left* for right handed throwers) executes the first part of its outwards rotation on its heel, and completes the second half – an inwards rotation – on its toe. The other foot leaves the ground at the beginning of the turn, and regains contact, alongside the turning foot, at the end of it.

DELIVERY
The hammer is worked downwards at the completion of the turns, then heaved away over the *leading* shoulder.

KEY POINTS

- Long, rhythmic swings
- Low point between the feet
- Straight arms
- Look at hammer head
- Balanced turning
- Stretch release.

PREPARATORY ACTIVITIES

EQUIPMENT
1 to 3kg medicine balls – one between two.

ORGANISATION
Open space, either at the centre of the track, along the kerb of the straight, or along a games pitch boundary line.

PROGRESSIONS
1. Take up a straddle stance, and make an underhand, backwards, overhead throw (fig T45) starting with the ball held between the legs. Keep long arms, and use a strong leg drive to heave the ball over the head.
   IP – Encourage throwers to follow through rather than remain fixed to the spot.

2. Make an 'over the shoulder' throw, starting from outside the hip (fig T46a) – *right* for right-handers, or *left* for left handers – and release over the other shoulder (fig T46b). Keep long arms, and twist the hips in the direction of throw as it is made.

Fig T45

Fig T46

a   b

3. Add a simple 'jump' turn (discus style) to the beginning of progression 2.
   Right-handed throwers pivot on the ball of the *left* foot, before jumping and making one full rotation to land, in a straddle stance, with back to the direction of throw, and with the implement back on the right side. Left-handed throwers work around the other way. Right handers continue the rotation into a lift and release over the shoulder. Left handers work vice versa.
4. Place the medicine ball into a strong sack, grip the 'neck' of the sack, and throw sack and ball in the same way as described in stage 3.
5. Competition is possible, and useful at each stage.

TEACHING PROGRESSIONS

EQUIPMENT
A selection of 3.25kg, 4kg or 5kg hammers, ideally sufficient for one per athlete, or failing that one between two or three is needed. A special hammer for teaching purposes can be made by unfastening the wire at the handle, taking it through the hole in the spindle and refastening the free end to the handle. This halves the overall length of the implement.

ORGANISATION
It is possible to teach a group safely, without use of a safety cage, if they are spread out in a line, as for discus, particularly when the special half length hammer is used. Obviously sufficient space needs to be kept between adjacent throwers, and when sharing implements, those not actually throwing at the time must stand well clear, to the rear, and watch the throwers. Again all throw, on the coach's command – then ALL retrieve together at the coach's second command.

THOSE IN CHARGE MUST BE ESPECIALLY WATCHFUL, ALERT AND CARING.

PROGRESSIONS

Fig T47

Stage One

1. THE HOLD – The handle is placed along the base of the fingers of the *left* hand of right-handed throwers, or vice versa for left-handers. The *other* hand covers that in contact with the handle (fig T47).

Stage Two

2. THE THROW – Take up a straddle stance, with feet shoulder width apart, facing away from the direction of throw, and with the implement on the *right* hand side – *left* for left-handers.

Stage Three

3. THROW AFTER SWING – Repeat stage 2, beginning with a 'pendulum' swing in which the hammer is given momentum by lifting it to eye level on straight arms, and then letting it drop back to its starting position, before slinging it over the *other* shoulder.

4. STANDING THROW – By now a simple standing throw will have been learned. Competition hereafter is thus the order of the day. This is a most suitable event for both boys and girls in the 13 and 14 year old age groups.
INVOLVE THEM IN THROWING, AND LET THE FEELING FOR THE EVENT DEVELOP.

Stage Four

5. TURNING – This skill needs to be taught before the event can progress further. Throwers start in the standing throw position (stage 3) with their *left* foot turned 90° to the left, and the heel raised off the ground. After one pendulum swing they jump turn around it as in preparatory stage 3. The *right* foot lands before the left. Delivery takes place after landing.

PLACE THE NEW SKILL INTO A COMPETITION AND ALLOW TIME FOR CONSOLIDATION.

Fig T48

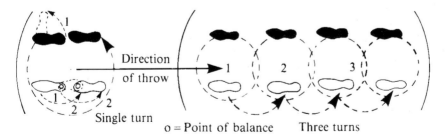

Single turn   o = Point of balance   Three turns

Stage Five

6. THE TURNING THROW – Satisfying distances and feelings come from learning how to turn, and incorporating the skill into the throw. The footwork (fig T48) needs to be drilled without the hammer in the following way:
   (i) Start in a straddle stance, with back towards the direction of throw, and *left* foot on a line drawn on the ground.
   (ii) Pivot simultaneously on the heel of the turning foot, and the ball of the other, until the turning foot has moved through 180° and is again pointing along the line, *but now in the direction of throw* (fig T49g-i).
   (iii) Transfer weight onto the ball of the turning foot (fig T49i).
   (iv) Complete the turn on the ball of the turning foot (fig T49i-k) picking the other foot off the ground and moving it around and outside the turning leg, until the starting attitude has been restored. In this way one turn will have been completed, and the thrower will have moved one foot length in the direction of throw.
7. Drill several successive turns, seeking for good balance throughout. These drills can also be practised using a broom shank or light rod held across the shoulders, or carried in front of the body on outstretched arms.
8. ADDING SWINGS TO THE TURNS – Make two swings around the head (see Basic Technical Model) followed by one turn. Stop suddenly and release over the *left* shoulder.
9. MAKING UP TWO TURNS – Add a further turn to the stage 8 sequence and throw.
10. MAKING UP THREE TURNS – Simply add a further turn to the sequence.
    This is now proper hammer throwing.

Fig T49

COMPLETE HAMMER THROW

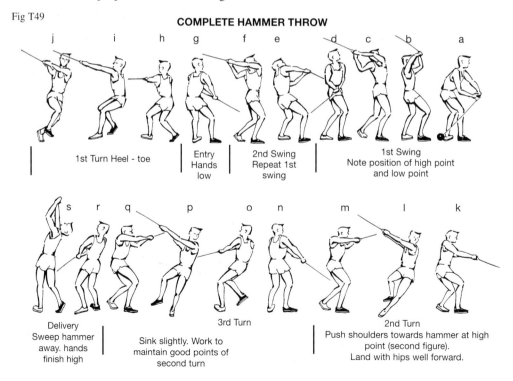

j   i   h   g   f   e   d   c   b   a

| 1st Turn Heel - toe | Entry Hands low | 2nd Swing Repeat 1st swing | 1st Swing Note position of high point and low point |

s   r   q   p   o   n   m   l   k

Delivery
Sweep hammer
away. hands
finish high

3rd Turn
Sink slightly. Work to
maintain good points of
second turn

2nd Turn
Push shoulders towards hammer at high
point (second figure).
Land with hips well forward.

GROUP ORGANISATION AND SAFETY FOR THROWING EVENTS

PROVISION

Ideally each child in a working group should have access to an implement for him/herself, which is appropriate to their special needs at that particular time. To equip a club or a school in this way can be a costly exercise. Fortunately it need not happen overnight. Acceptable improvisations are possible such as:

- shot from stones
- shot from pellets encased in old nylon stockings
- discoi from soft wood plates fastened together (fig T50)
- hoops or quoits used as discoi
- javelins made from cane or dowel and hosepipe (fig T51)
- cricket balls, hockey balls or shuttlecocks used as javelins
- hammers from chain, rope, and hosepipe (fig T52), quoits (fig T53) or by placing large balls or medicine balls into sacks or plastic bags.

Fig T50

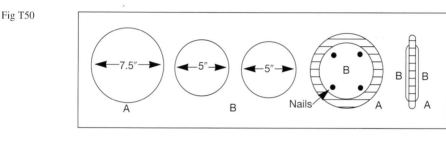

Fig T51

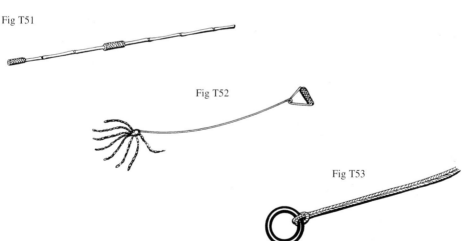

Fig T52

Fig T53

WHERE SUCH PRIVATE IMPROVISATIONS ARE USED IT IS ESSENTIAL THAT THEY ARE INHERENTLY SAFE IN THEIR CONSTRUCTION, AND CONSTANTLY CHECKED FOR SAFETY DURING USE.

STORAGE

The integrity of throwing implements is best maintained when they are stored in an organised way. This preserves their safety in use. Shot, discoi and javelins are best placed in specially constructed racks. In this way their numbers can be easily checked. Hammers are best hung from individual hooks so that the wires remain on constant stretch. It is useful to spend a bit of time with paint spray cans and to colour code implements of different weights or sizes for easy identification.

Racks for heavier implements, such as shot, should be placed on the floor, or low down, so that they can't accidentally drop on people's feet when being removed or returned. Javelins are best stored vertically. PE small apparatus such as balls, quoits, bean bags ought to be stored in small apparatus baskets or bins.

TRANSPORT

When moving apparatus from the store to the place of use a decision has to be made as to whether or not one uses specially selected monitors to carry in bulk, or for each child in the group to collect their own. The first method avoids the involvement of unreliable people who could cause accidents, but poses difficulties when heavy implements such as shot or hammers are involved. Even javelins, which are the lightest throwing implements, pose problems because of their size and shape. Special trolleys for storage and transport can be obtained, but they are not cheap. Javelins should always be carried vertically, point down, in front of the carrier.

IN USE

Before any throwing takes place the person in charge should make sure that:
- all implements have been checked, and shown to be safe to use
- that those who may be awaiting their turn to throw do so in a safe place, and at a safe distance, and
- that people control the implements in their possession, particularly javelins which are best either laid on the ground, or stuck firmly and vertically into it.

  During throwing those in charge should ensure that:
- each THROWER assumes personal responsibility for ensuring that the landing area is clear before he or she makes their throw (even if others have indicated that it is)
- are retrieved ONLY after all in the group have thrown
- participants NEVER run when carrying implements
- participants NEVER run to collect a javelin
- javelins are pushed into a VERTICAL position before being pulled VERTICALLY from the ground.

  Where large groups are involved an adult must assume absolute control.

  When implements have to be shared the change over is accident prone. The chance that one child may accidentally drop one onto another's foot must be avoided. There are two standard ways of doing this:
- The retriever places the implement on the ground, and the next user picks it up, or
- the next user retrieves the implement – NOT the thrower.

SELF DISCIPLINE IS AN ESSENTIAL COMPONENT OF SAFE THROWS LEARNING AND PRACTICE.

INSTRUCTIONAL ORGANISATION

INSTRUCTION IN BASIC AND INTRODUCTORY ACTIVITIES AWAY FROM SAFETY
CAGES REMAINS COMMON PRACTICE.

It is perfectly safe provided extra care is taken to ensure that participants are safely arranged and
spaced. The rotational events, such as discus and hammer, require more space between adjacent
individuals (say 6 – 8 metres) whereas shot and javelin which are linear in nature can get by
safely with closer spacing such as 2 – 4 metres. Figures T54 to T60 show the more commonly
used group arrangements for throwing.

Fig T54 shows an arrangement by which a group of 30 can be accommodated working in a
straight line. Because this is a long arrangement, coach/teacher contact and control is thus
diminished. It requires the group to be called in each time that something needs to be said to all,
so breaks up the activity. Use of a megaphone gets round this problem.

Fig T55 overcomes the contact and control weakness of the T54 arrangement but reduces the
number of throws which can be made by each participant.

Fig T56 is good for discus practice because it places most throwers behind those on their left,
and reduces risk of injury resulting from a 'sliced' throw. Left-handed throwers take up positions
at the left end of the line. In this arrangement the construction of distance guide lines is not easy,
although not impossible.

Fig T57 in which the throwers are lined up in echelon offers the same advantages for discus
throwing as the arrangement around a curve. Left-handed throwers take up positions to the left
of the line. Accurate estimations of the distance thrown is not easy, and in practice there is a

Fig T54

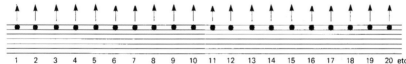

Fig T55

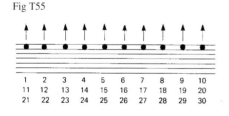

Fig T56

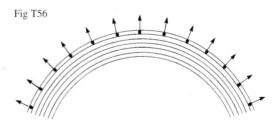

Fig T57

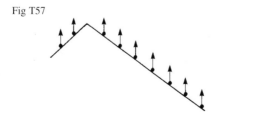

Fig T58   Fig T59

Fig T60

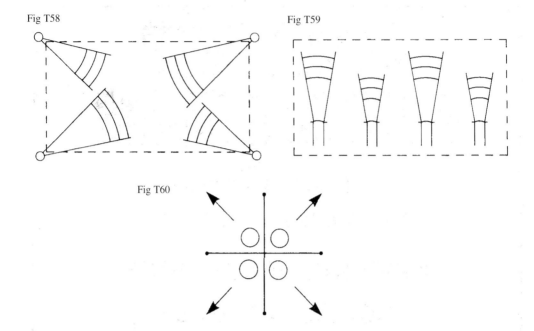

tendency for throwers to revert to throwing at right angles to the throw line, and thereby nullify the safety advantages of the system.

PRACTICE ORGANISATION

Having been taught a particular throwing skill children need time alone in which to practise it, and space in which to do this safely. A child working alone is unlikely either to be injured, or to injure another. Such provision ought to be the ultimate aim of all involved in teaching or coaching throwing events. It can be relatively easily attained. Figures T58 to T60 show some ways of achieving this, using facilities such as games pitches or basic, easily constructed safety cages.

Fig T 58 shows a way of using a games pitch to provide four, safe sites for long throws made from circles.

Fig T59 shows a way of using a similar pitch to provide four safe javelin throwing areas. The alternate use of distance arcs, indicating long distances and short distances adjacent to one another encourages throwers to be selective of where they work, and creates greater safety where the implement is expected to land.

Fig T60 utilises a simple inexpensive cage, which since it is a safety provision only for those around it, need not be more than 2.50 metres high. It can accommodate safe group work by arranging for non-throwers to await their turn in one bay, whilst the other three are in use.

FEEDBACK

KNOWLEDGE OF THE DISTANCE THROWN IS AN IMPORTANT FACTOR IN THE SUCCESS STAKES.

It is more efficient, and more effective, to have distance lines permanently marked on the ground, at suitable intervals, than to measure each throw.